T0329262

ALL SAINTS' CHURCH
HORSEHEATH

Alington Monument, 1613.

ALL SAINTS' CHURCH
HORSEHEATH

CATHERINE E. PARSONS

Cambridge
at the University Press
1911

CAMBRIDGE
UNIVERSITY PRESS

University Printing House, Cambridge CB2 8BS, United Kingdom

Cambridge University Press is part of the University of Cambridge.

It furthers the University's mission by disseminating knowledge in the pursuit of education, learning and research at the highest international levels of excellence.

www.cambridge.org
Information on this title: www.cambridge.org/9781107594197

© Cambridge University Press 1911

First published 1911
First paperback edition 2015

A catalogue record for this publication is available from the British Library

ISBN 978-1-107-59419-7 Paperback

CONTENTS

---

* This map is available for download from www.cambridge.org/9781107594197

CORRECTION

On p. 95. The statement as to the Rev. W. Battiscombe's Sunday journeys to London is, I find, not true and should be omitted.

CHAPTER I

THE STRUCTURE

HORSEHEATH Church in the Deanery of Camps, Cambridgeshire, is built upon a site which we have reason to believe has been inhabited by man from very early times. We have found many specimens of Neolithic man's craft scattered over the fields in the parish. No Celtic remains have been discovered, but ample evidence of Roman occupation was yielded in 1910 by the author's excavations in a field called Hanging Hill, abutting upon Worsted Road, and the very name of Horseheath is of Saxon origin. Whether the Christian Saxons built a church at Horseheath we are unable to say.

In the Domesday Survey of Horsei, as Horseheath was then designated, no mention is made of a church, but, as the commissioners were not obliged to make any return of the churches, there is no significance in the omission. Although the formation of parishes—an organization for church purposes—began in Saxon times, we do not know when it was that Horseheath became a parish forming part of the diocese under the jurisdiction of the Bishop of Ely.

Probably the first stone church at Horseheath was built after the Norman Conquest, about the middle of the twelfth century. How funds were raised to build it, or who the founder was, are points shrouded in obscurity. The maintenance of the services, the repairs of the church fabric, or rebuilding, were, in early times, the sacred trust of the parishioners. No doubt the first church built of stone at Horseheath stood in the same position as the church of to-day—a position not without interest, a little to the south of Wool Street—frequently called the Roman road, and by the most extensive moated enclosure in the parish. This early church was perhaps of the simplest form, smaller than the present church and composed of nave and chancel, with no aisles, clerestory or tower, built of local flint, with chancel arch, windows and doorways of Barnack stone. In fact, the only distinctive architectural remains we have to-day of this early church are the pieces of Barnack stone, worked with the Norman zig-zag pattern, that are built into the walls of the present church. Three varieties of such zig-zag moulding may be seen in the interior of the nave walls. These pieces of stone would form part of the Norman church at Horseheath in which Guy de Burgh and Ralph Weaver took sanctuary in 1260[1] after they had killed Robert le Bode of Shudy Camps. Unfortunately these malefactors escaped from the church, and, in consequence, the villagers were fined.

Restorations, or alterations made in the Norman church during the thirteenth century, are exceedingly

[1] P. R. O. *Cambs. Assize Roll,* 82.

difficult matters to determine, and were it not for the
fragments of masonry which appear to have Early
English stops upon them at the bases of both the
chancel and tower arches, there is apparently nothing
to show that any work was done that might possibly
be attributed to the Early English period. We would
mention that these fragments of masonry, which somewhat resemble Early English work, at the base of the
tower arch, occur in conjunction with a piece of
Norman moulding, similar to that built into the walls
of the nave, some of which is near the roof, whilst
other pieces are near the foundation of the walls, so
that the position of the Norman worked stone does
not assist in determining Early English construction.
And we may perhaps assume that the Norman church
had little, if any, alteration effected during the Early
English period. In any case, the church to-day,
which is dedicated to All Saints, affords ample evidence
of such restoration which practically amounts to its
having been entirely rebuilt in the fourteenth century,
during the Decorated period.

When the rebuilding of Horseheath church in the
fourteenth century was completed, the ground-plan of
the chancel, nave, tower and south porch was the same
as that of to-day. (See plan.) The position of the
buttress by the north door of the nave, which now
forms part of the vestry, makes it improbable that
there was originally a north porch. And if we picture
a high-pitched roof on the nave, coming down lower
than the present roof, over smaller windows, the
external appearance of the church would probably
represent its original construction. The church is

chiefly built of flint, and, as will be seen by the plan, the tower has suffered less from restoration than any other part of the church. It is embattled with stone, and is divided by three string courses, the lower one of which on the east face marks the high-pitched roof of the fourteenth century nave. Perhaps the chief points of interest in the tower are the newel staircase, the two fine gargoyles on the north and south faces— ornamented with grotesque heads of animals, and the drip-stones terminated by the head of a man and the head of a woman over the windows in the upper storey. The drip-stone over the west window in the belfry has the same terminals. The tracery in this window is a good example of Decorated work.

Although the south porch has suffered a good deal from restoration, the fourteenth century windows and inner doorway still remain. It is a curious coincidence that a piscina has been placed in this porch in the position of a holy water stoup. This piscina may originally have been in the nave in mediaeval days, when there would most likely have been an altar on either side of the chancel arch. The piscina for the altar on the south still remains, and, although it has been restored, the Barnack basin is evidently of the fourteenth century. Possibly here, if not on the north side of the chancel arch, was the chapel of Our Blessed Lady, to which chapel, John Pettit of Horseheath, in his will dated 1512[1], bequeathed a cow for keeping a light for ever. The sedilia in the chapel on the south are of the plainest.

[1] *Cons. Court of Ely*, Vol. E. f. 75.

The north and east portions of the chancel are work of the Decorated period. In the subsequent restorations on the south portion of the chancel, the same style of architecture has been retained. The principal feature in the chancel during the fourteenth century was the stone High Altar. Seats or stalls would be provided in the chancel for the officiating clergy, and also a seat for the patron, then the Earl of Oxford. The chancel was probably divided from the nave by a beam on which the rood was placed.

The fourteenth century nave with its high-pitched roof, its smaller windows, altars on either side of the chancel arch, and the spacious floor strewn with rushes or straw, without pews, is now changed almost out of recognition. There would undoubtedly have been wall paintings, and painted glass in some of the windows, in fact one of the most interesting relics preserved in the church to-day is the small shield, checky, argent and sable[1], impaling gules, fretty, or, a bordure, argent, semée de fleur-de-lis, sable, for Audley, which family held one of the three manors in Horseheath during the fourteenth century.

Practically all the alterations effected in the structure of the church during the fifteenth century were confined to the nave. The high-pitched roof was replaced by the present flat roof, and the walls were raised to suit it. The large windows of six lights were inserted, and were probably soon enriched with coloured glass. It is possible that the fifteenth century, or Perpendicular roof, was originally built with a stone battlemented

[1] This coat occurs in the arms of the Priory, Austin Canons, at Royston, Herts.

parapet, for the present brick parapet is of much more recent date, and certainly not the parapet towards the repair of which Robert Pettit of Horseheath, in his will dated 1524[1], bequeathed the sum of forty shillings. Some of the carving on the interior of the roof at the west end of the nave is still preserved. Cole tells us that, in 1742[2], in the centre of the roof there were the arms of the Bishopric of Ely carved, gules, three ducal coronets, or; probably these arms, and most of the other carving, disappeared when the roof was repaired in 1764. The tower and chancel arches were raised during the fifteenth century, and the fine wooden screen was put in the chancel arch. This screen has been well preserved, and retains traces of colour on the panels of a conventional floral design, in red and white. Over the screen in the fifteenth century was the rood-loft, upon which stood the great rood or crucifix with the attendant images of S. Mary and S. John. The rood-loft staircase has entirely disappeared, but the upper and lower doorways, at the most easterly corner of the north wall of the nave, still remain. The carved spandrils of the arch in the lower doorway are good, that on the dexter side represents a cross proceeding from a heart, a somewhat unusual design.

The octagonal font at the west end of the nave is also a good piece of fifteenth century work. (See illustration.) The basin is of Barnack stone, whilst clunch is used for the pedestal, where less durability is required. Clunch, we should mention, was also

---

[1] *Addit. MS.* 5861, f. 177.
[2] *Addit. MS.* 5802.

The Font, Horseheath Church.

used for the raising of the tower and chancel arches, for the nave windows, the rood-loft doorways, and for the restoration of the piscina by the altar on the south of the chancel arch. This piscina has a crocketed ogee hood-moulding over the niche. Another piece of fifteenth century work is the Purbeck marble altar tomb (see page 39), of which we have been able to give a conjectural drawing from the broken fragments discovered in the Rectory garden, forming part of a rockery. It is possible that the original position of this tomb was in the south chapel.

Probably seats for the congregation were first introduced in the nave when the fifteenth century alterations were effected, though the days of high pews had not yet come.

At the present time there is an entire absence of painted glass in the nave windows, except for the few fragments that are used indiscriminately. Nothing however remains of the subjects that formerly adorned the fine Perpendicular windows in the nave, some of which subjects were still in existence when Cole visited the church in 1742. Therefore, we attribute the loss of the painted glass in Horseheath Church to the hand of the nineteenth century restorer, rather than to any destruction wrought at the time of the Reformation, when, it appears, little was done to disfigure the so-called superstitious pictures in the windows. In one of the north windows, in 1695[1], there remained beneath some good coloured glass the words "propitietur Deus Amen A° Dn° M° CCCC." This was certainly some of

---

[1] *Harleian MS.* 6821, f. 50.

the original glass, put in after the fifteenth century alterations. From Cole's account of the glass in 1742[1], we find, that, in the middle lower light of the north window in the nave next the chancel arch, there was a large picture of the Blessed Virgin with *Stã Maria* at her feet. This figure was perfect except that the head was missing. In the other five lights of this window, there were pictures representing stories from the New Testament. One representing the Lord's Supper being almost perfect. There were also in this same window two shields which bore the arms of the patron, the Earl of Oxford. Quarterly, gules and or, with a mullet in the first quarter. Cole remarks that altogether there were no less than seven shields in the windows which bore these same arms. Fragments of these shields have been inserted in the east window in the chancel. In the middle window of the nave, on the north, there were several pictures of saints, but the upper part of them had gone, and in the lower centre light of this window, there was a shield bearing the arms, baron and femme, 1st the four usual bearings of the Alingtons, but the 3rd and 4th quarters were broken, and filled with other glass. The 1st and 2nd remained, namely Alington, sable, a bend engrailed between twelve billets, argent; and Argentine, gules, three covered cups, argent, impaling barry of six or eight, ermine and gules. This shield represented the arms of William Alington and his wife Elizabeth, whose monumental slab now lies within the chancel arch. In the window on the north, next the tower, there were the remains of two saints, and

---

[1] *Addit. MS.* 5802.

a shield with the same quartering for Alington and Argentine. As the description of the subjects in the other north windows given by Cole is fairly complete, perhaps this is the north window in which the words and date "propitietur Deus Amen A° Dn° M° CCCC..." occurred in 1695. In the nave window on the south, next the chancel, Cole says there was some good old painted glass, and in this window a few fragments still remain. The arms of William and Elizabeth Alington above mentioned were also in this window, and in the middle window on the south. Surely the repetition of these arms points to the fact that William Alington and his wife, as well as the Earl of Oxford, the patron of the living, must have contributed largely towards the fifteenth century alterations. In the window next the tower on the south, Cole says there was no painted glass at all.

The structure of the chancel, tower and south porch remained untouched during the fifteenth century. In the sixteenth century apparently no structural alterations were made to Horseheath Church, although in the interior many changes took place. Such changes, that made it many years before the parishioners could reduce their church to a state of order, since much in our churches that was destroyed under King Edward VI was again restored for a short time during Queen Mary's reign. In the first year of Queen Elizabeth's reign similar injunctions to those of King Edward VI were enforced, the result being a period of general dilapidation. Perhaps the first important alteration in the interior of the church would be the destruction of the rood with the images in 1541. After the destruction of the rood, rendering the rood doorways and staircase—important features in the fifteenth century—useless, the Royal Arms were set up on the mural screen, in place of the rood. It was in 1569 that an enquiry was issued as to whether rood-lofts had been pulled down, so that if the rood had been set up in Horseheath Church in Queen Mary's reign, it did not long survive. An edict went forth in 1550 that all stone altars were to be destroyed, and in their place one Communion Table was to be provided, so that beside the removal of the High Altar at the east end of the chancel—the place where it had stood had not been whitewashed by the neglect of the church-wardens in 1561[1]—the side altars in the nave, would also be removed. Mural paintings would be obliterated at this time, and probably texts of scripture were then painted in their place. Therefore, the interior of the church was considerably changed in the sixteenth century. An interesting feature of this century's work is the sundial on the south porch, which bears the date 1566.

The records referring to Horseheath Church in the early part of the seventeenth century reveal a state of general neglect. In 1643[2] things were made worse by a visit from William Dowsing, a Suffolk man, who, under order of a Parliamentary Commission, signed by the Earl of Manchester, undertook to effect certain reforms in Cambridgeshire churches. William Dowsing was ordered to take away or deface all crucifixes, images of the Virgin Mary, or images of

[1] Ely, 'Comperta' of *Bp. Cox* 1561.
[2] Carter's *History of Cambridgeshire*.

the Trinity, pictures of saints, superstitious pictures, and superstitious inscriptions. Spoliation was the object of the visit, with the hope of suppressing superstition. According to William Dowsing's journal, on 5th January, 1643, he visited Horseheath Church, and broke down two crucifixes, and destroyed four pictures of the prophets Daniel, Zachariah, Malachi, Ezekiel and Sophany and two more, with forty superstitious pictures. This entry makes lamentable reading, but, as we have already seen, some of the pictures, although disfigured, were not destroyed, as in the case of the figure of the Virgin in one of the north windows in the nave. Neither were the so-called superstitious inscriptions defaced on the monumental slabs, as will be seen later on.

We believe that it was later on in the seventeenth century, when episcopal jurisdiction had been restored, that the interior of Horseheath Church was made neat according to the then prevailing fashion, with plaster and whitewash. The rood-loft staircase was removed, the rood-loft doorways were blocked up and plastered over. The tower arch was blocked up, and a chamber for the bell-ringers was made, by putting a floor in the tower midway up the tower arch, the lower part of the arch was boarded and had a door inserted, the upper part of the arch was filled in with masonry. The windows in the south porch may have been blocked up about this time, making it somewhat dark for those who had business to transact in the church porch, where, formerly, there were oak plank seats on either side. The gallery at the west end of the nave was probably erected in the seventeenth century, and also the large canopied oak pew 9 ft. × 6 ft., with panelled roof and sides, and carved entablature. This pew originally stood in the southeast corner of the nave. It is now in private hands.

At the end of the seventeenth century, or about the beginning of the eighteenth, red brick was freely used in the structural restoration of the church. The present red brick embattled parapet was put on the nave. An unsightly brick buttress was built on the south of the chancel, and the south porch was restored in red brick. The red brick vestry on the north of the nave would probably be built about this time, and from the fact of its having originally had an outer doorway, we think that it may once have served as a north porch, and that the doorway was blocked up, and the window inserted, when first used as a vestry. In 1787[1] the interior of the vestry was so dilapidated that it was almost useless.

The red brick dormitory, measuring twenty-five feet by fourteen, on the north of the chancel, was built in 1711. A faculty for its erection was granted to John Bromley, Esq., the then lord of the manor of Horseheath, by James Johnson, vicar-general to John, Bishop of Ely, on 22nd August 1711[2]. This dormitory or mortuary chapel was entered by a door beneath the chancel window. It had become dilapidated in 1783. Happily this unsightly erection was taken down in 1829 by Lord Montfort's permission. The coffins which belonged to Lord Montfort's family were placed in a vault beneath the chancel in October 1828.

---

[1] *Rural Dean's Returns*, B. 7.   [2] *Addit. MS.* 5823, f. 79.

Horseheath Church from North-East.

After the exterior restoration of the church in red brick, the interior was redecorated. Cole[1] tells us that an inscription to this effect was painted on the wall of the nave over the belfry arch, surrounded by a floral border—" Repaired and Beautified Anno Domini 1721. John Slaney and Joseph Wakefield, churchwardens." According to the prevailing taste, the decoration of Horseheath Church must have been highly improved at this time. Over the north door the Apostles' Creed was painted in a yellow frame, formed by festoons of fruit and flowers, painted in yellow, with angels in various attitudes supporting them. Beneath the Creed were the words in Greek Ἐπιθυμοῦσιν ἄγγελοι παρακύψαι 1 S. Peter i. 12.

Over the south door, the Lord's Prayer was painted in a similar style to match the Creed, and on the wall on either side of the chancel arch there were the Ten Commandments painted with the same kind of artistic framing. In fact, the whole of the church walls were adorned with texts and festoons of fruit and flowers supported by angels.

At this time the high wainscot pulpit, hung with purple cloth, with fringe to match, its sounding-board above and the clerk's seat below, stood by the north wall of the nave, between the two most easterly windows. The floor of the nave was laid with red and white brick, and the chancel, and north and south porch, with tiles.

The restoration or repair of the Perpendicular roof was not apparently undertaken until the year 1764.

[1] *Addit. MS.* 5802.

This is the date carved on the timber at the east end, together with the initials of the then churchwardens, J[ohn] T[winn] and J[ohn] S[wan]. Beside the churchwardens' initials there is a W. B. carved— probably the initials of the builder, since Philip Bearcroft was then rector of Horseheath.

In 1783[1] the church is described as dirty. There was a brick arch out of repair and three rows of seats in the nave were evidently unsafe. The tiling and walls were reported to be in a fair state of repair.

There is little to say about the chancel in the eighteenth century. It must have been very dark, since the two large Alington monuments excluded all light from the most easterly windows, north and south. On either side of the chancel there were two pews with doors. There was a wooden altar rail and balusters, with a gate to match. The Communion Table then in use is probably that which now stands in the vestry. Cole tells us that the roof of the chancel was handsomely vaulted and whitewashed, and that it had several ornaments of fleur-de-lis and roses in stucco upon it. This ornamentation has now all disappeared. In 1787[2] the chancel was particularly cold owing to the door gaping, a defect which had been endured for four years. Ultimately a suggested remedy was that the door should be lined with thin wood, so as to improve the appearance, as well as making the chancel warmer.

Considerable alterations were made in the nave of the church between the year 1721, when it was

[1] *Rural Dean's Returns*, B. 7.
[2] *Id.*

repaired and beautified, and the year 1891, when it was reduced to its present state. At the beginning of the nineteenth century there was great difficulty in getting the ordinary repairs of the church done. In 1823 there was only one churchwarden, as the other appointed had refused to take the oath, and so was incompetent to act[1]. The one acting churchwarden, Joseph Lawrence, had been lax in making a rate for church repairs. To him the Archdeacon wrote on 22nd October 1823, requesting him to lose no time in putting the church into a complete state of repair. The tower was to be examined. The timber in the belfry was to be repaired, and something was to be done to prevent the rain coming through the leads on the roof. The battlements were to be repaired wherever they were dilapidated, and two casements were to be put in windows on the north and south of the nave for ventilation. In August 1824[2] none of these matters had received attention, no rate had been levied, and correspondence continued between the Archdeacon and the harassed curate; the rector was non-resident. Law empowered the churchwarden to make a rate for necessary repairs, not exceeding ten pounds at any time, and to obtain a warrant of distress against anyone who refused to pay, so by the intervention of this Act it was hoped to accomplish much by degrees. In 1825 a resident rector held the Horseheath living and by a letter from the Deputy Registrar addressed to him, we see how matters progressed.

[1] *Papers at Horseheath Rectory.*   [2] *Id.*

ARCHDEACONRY OFFICE,
CAMBRIDGE.
30 *December* 1826.

SIR[1],

By the direction of the Reverend the Official of the Archdeaconry of Ely, I beg leave to reply to your Letter of the 23rd instant addressed to him respecting the reduction of the Bells in the parish church of Horseheath. On the 22nd Sept. 1824 a Citation issued under the Archdeaconry seal calling upon the churchwardens of the parish of Horseheath to show cause why the parish church had been allowed to go into decay, and why various repairs should not immediately be done (enumerating them). On the 16th Oct. 1824 the day of the return of the citation the Court made the following order. "That the churchwardens give a Bond to the Office of the Registrar to complete the repairs as stated in the annexed report of Mr Hayles. And that the fourth and fifth Bells be recast so as to make one Bell of a tone suitable to the other three. And that the repairs mentioned in the further part of the Citation be entirely completed within three months from this day. Dated this 16th day of October 1824."

I am, Sir,

Your very obed[t] Servant,

G. B. WHITE,
Dep[y] Registrar.

[1] *Papers at Horseheath Rectory.*

Precisely when it was that the condition of the church was brought about, as remembered by many of the Horseheath parishioners of to-day, before the restoration of the chancel in 1883, and the restoration of the nave in 1891, is a difficult matter to determine. Previous to these restorations, the church had lost much of the adornment it possessed in the early part of the previous century. The chancel ceiling had been plastered, without any attempt of decoration further than whitewash, and, at the sacrifice of the canopy of the handsome Alington monument, the south window in the chancel has been re-opened and glazed, in order to give more light in the chancel. The opposite window on the north still remains blocked up by the monument on that side.

The festoons of fruit and flowers had disappeared, and the Commandments had been painted at the end of the nave, on either side of the chancel arch, in black lettering on a yellowish or buff ground, finished by a narrow brown border. A small portion of this border may still be seen by the piers of the chancel arch. The high pulpit with its sounding-board and clerk's seat had been removed from the north wall to the position of the present unsightly stone pulpit.

The chancel was repaired in 1829[1]. Owing to the earth outside the chancel being two or three feet above the level of the floor, the chancel was very damp. This earth was removed in 1829, and the floor was raised eight inches. The bell chamber floor was also repaired in 1829.

[1] Ely, *Visitation Articles and Returns*, C. 2.

It may have been about this time that the reputed canopied pew on the north of the chancel arch disappeared, for it is said that there was one of these pews on either side of the chancel arch. In any case a high deal pew was more recently put in the northeast corner of the nave, between the pulpit and the rood doorway. Except for the oak canopied pew on the south, and two oak benches parallel with the south wall—in later years reserved for the aged men who were unable to mount the gallery stairs—the whole of the nave was fitted with high deal pews provided with doors. Some of them were lined with red or green baize. One, we remember, was lined with red baize stamped with a black fleur-de-lis, with hassocks, or to use a local word, pesses, to match. The seats beneath the gallery were raised one above the other, a step or two being provided as required by the height of the seats. The early fifteenth century font still retained its position between these raised blocks of seats. Although the earth which lay round the chancel walls had been removed in 1829, the damp state of the chancel was still a source of trouble in 1876, in which year the then rector applied for a faculty for making considerable alterations in the chancel, but as this rector vacated the Horseheath living about the time the faculty was granted, the alterations, at an estimated cost of six hundred pounds, were never carried out. The petition for the faculty, dated 3rd April, 1875[1], states that the chancel required restoration and repair, and that a new vestry was needed. This was to have been built on the south

---

[1] *Ely Diocesan Registrary.*

of the chancel, and also a chamber for the organ. Recesses were to have been built for the Alington monuments. The roof was to be reconstructed. The defective north wall was to have been repaired, and the plaster work was also. The choir seats were to have been lengthened, and additional choir seats provided. The floor of the chancel was to have been relaid with tiles, and a new step made. An oak Communion Table, and a reredos of stone and encaustic figured tiles, were also to have been provided. Towards the expense of these alterations the sum of two hundred and ninety-five pounds had been paid over to the Governors of Queen Anne's Bounty by the executors of the late rector, in accordance with the Dilapidations Act. The remainder of the six hundred pounds was to have been raised by public subscription. The defective north wall here mentioned would probably be where the Bromley mortuary chapel had previously stood. The vestry still remains in a dilapidated condition, and a suitable place for the organ has yet to be found.

Soon after the granting of this faculty for restoration, trenches were dug round the foundations of the chancel in order to make it drier, but it was not until 1883 that the chancel was restored, at a cost of about four hundred pounds. It was then the plaster ceiling was taken down, the timber was replaned, and the roof thoroughly repaired and retiled. The south wall was taken down and rebuilt from the foundation, and the walls on the interior of the chancel were replastered. New stone was put in the south windows, the design of the tracery being kept the same as in the old

windows. The east window was restored. The
windows on the north of the chancel are original.
One of these, as we have already mentioned, is blocked
up by an Alington monument. On the window
which is glazed there is neatly written, "John Pendle,
Linton, May 16, 1883. Forget me not, glazer."
It was also in 1883 that the piscina in the chancel was
restored, and that the present altar, altar rail, and choir
seats were provided. The screen was taken down
and sent to Cambridge to be cleaned and repaired, and
was happily replaced in its original position.

On the whole the chancel restoration of 1883 is
more pleasant to contemplate than the restoration of
the nave in 1891, when, at a cost of over four hundred
pounds the west gallery was taken down, and the wainscot pulpit discarded. The clerk's seat and sounding-
board had previously disappeared. All the high pews
were removed, including the large oak-canopied pew.
The plaster was taken off the walls, and with it the
Commandments. The rood-loft doorways, however,
were again exposed to view, and also several pieces
of Norman moulding, when the walls were replastered.
The brick floor gave place to the present one of wood-
blocks. The pitch-pine benches were introduced.
Ten pounds towards their cost, and the repairing of
the church, were given by the Incorporated Church
Building Society. A notice-board to this effect is in
the church. It states that one hundred and eighty-
four seats are for the free use of the parishioners
according to law. In 1865 there were one hundred
and eight appropriated sittings in the church, and one
hundred and thirty-seven non-appropriated sittings,

in addition to seventy-six sittings for children. The population of Horseheath then being four hundred and ninety-seven, two hundred and nine of which population attended church.

The organ, which had formerly stood in the centre of the gallery, was removed to its present position. (See plan.) It was during the alterations of 1891 that the belfry arch was opened, and that the oak door now in the belfry was made from one of the old oak seats formerly reserved for the aged men. We remember the hat-rail fitted with large pegs, provided for these seats.

The south porch was restored in 1894, when an entirely new roof was put on at a cost of fifteen pounds. The windows were reopened, and the red brick arch of the seventeenth or eighteenth century restoration was replaced by the present stone arch. The wooden gates to the porch were removed at this time. The oak benches had long since disappeared.

CHAPTER II

CHURCH FURNITURE

UNDER this heading we will consider such things in connection with Horseheath Church that do not form part of the structure itself, such as the church plate, books, vestments, bells and ornaments. And when we remember the wealth of the pre-Reformation Church and the character of the services, so specially adapted to a display of artistic wealth, it is not surprising to find that our earliest inventories of church goods are more interesting than subsequent inventories.

The earliest inventory we have of Horseheath Church goods dates from the beginning of the fourteenth century, when there were usually three services on Sundays and Holy Days : Mattins at six or seven o'clock a.m., High Mass at nine a.m., and Evensong at any time from two p.m. to three p.m.

The priest said his office of Mattins, Prime and Terce before Mass on Sundays and Holy Days, and a sermon occasionally accompanied the Mass. A daily Mass was said, sometimes as early as four o'clock in the morning. For these services eight different kinds of service-books were necessary for the use of the officiating clergy. These service-books were usually provided by the parishioners, and being hand-written, probably on vellum, with beautifully engrossed initial letters, and handsomely bound, were in themselves a valuable possession of the parish church. Even the old and incomplete volumes are enumerated in an inventory of Horseheath Church goods. By this inventory[1], made in 1300, we find that one of the necessary books, the Ordinal, was missing. This book contained the proper offices for the year. The seven different kinds of service-books which occur in the inventory are: 1. A Missal, used for Mass; 2. A Legend, containing the lessons for Mattins; 3. An Antiphonary, the music book for the canonical hours with 4. a Psalter, 5. a Grail which provided the music for the liturgy of the Mass; 6. A Troper which contained the music for the non-Gregorian turns of music and words, interpolated in the text of the Liturgy; 7. A Manual. This book contained the occasional Offices, that is to say, the services for baptism, marriage, visitation of the sick, churching of women, and burial of the dead. Probably this particular Manual was the copy still in use at Horseheath in the year 1379, to which reference is made in the Proof of Age[2] of William Sybill, of Horseheath, taken in 1401, when a certain John Lynton gives evidence that he held the book near the Chaplain at the baptism of the said William, which took place on the Feast of the Blessed Virgin Mary, 1379. Amongst other witnesses to this baptism there was

[1] Bodleian, *Rawlinson MS.* B. f. 20.
[2] *Inq. Post Mortem*, 3 Henry IV, No. 55.

John Norfolk, who remembered the occasion because he carried the basin and towel to the church for the ceremony. At this time it was required by law that every church should be provided with a chalice and paten. From this early inventory of goods, we find that Horseheath Church possessed two of these. A pyx, the vessel that hung before the High Altar, which contained the reserved sacrament, is mentioned in this same inventory, and also two censers, three cruets for Holy Oils, and two crosses. One of these crosses would be for processional use. A cross, we are told, was not a usual ornament for an altar at so early a date.

The Lenten Veil, which hung between the chancel and the nave from the evening before the first Sunday in Lent till the Thursday before Easter, is included in the inventory. And in addition to the one set of vestments required by law, including an amice, alb, girdle, stole, maniple, dalmatic and chasuble, there were three other sets, seven surplices, a rochet, and three cushions. These cushions, and a rochet, were presented to the church by Simon de Nosterfield, rector of Horseheath[1].

An interesting inventory of Horseheath Church goods was made in 1552[2]. It was the outcome of a Royal Commission whose business it was to find out, as precisely as possible, what wealth the Church possessed, what goods were superfluous under the injunctions of King Edward VI, and what could reasonably be sold in order to provide funds for the King. The Commissioners came to Horseheath on

[1] *Rawl. MS.* B. f. 20.
[2] P. R. O. *Augmentation Book*, 495, No. 114.

the fifth of August. They weighed the silver, made
a list of all the goods, carefully noting the material
of the vestments, and decided upon such things they
considered it necessary that the church should be
allowed to retain for the use of divine service. There
were two silver chalices, with their patens; one weighed
eleven and a quarter ounces, and the other ten ounces
and three quarters. The Commissioners left the heavier
of the two for the use of the church. The things they
took away, being superfluous and unnecessary for divine
service, were a gilded tin cross, two copper crosses, a
copper pyx, a latten 'schip,' four lead cruets, two
standing candlesticks, four smaller latten candlesticks,
a copper lamp and a pair of latten censers. These
objects, for many years sacred to the Horseheath
parishioners, scarcely have the same interest for us
that we justly attach to the beautiful embroidery and
woven materials included in this same inventory of
1552. There were a whole suit of blue silk, and a
blue baudekyn cope. This cope must have been exceedingly handsome, the baudekyn being composed of
blue silk, interwoven with threads of gold. There were
also a green baudekyn cope, and another of white
damask. There were a red damask vestment, and
one of purple silk, two small purple pillows or cushions,
which would be used for book supports, and a cloth to
hang before the altar of the same colour and material.
Also a similar cloth which was fringed. There were a
vestment of white silk and two white silk altar frontals,
a red silk vestment, and a red silk tunicle—the short
outer garment worn by a sub-deacon. There were a
green silk vestment, a knotted dornix vestment, a purple

dornix vestment, and another of blue and white dornix, which material, a coarse kind of damask, was originally made at Dorneck, the Dutch name for Tournay. This inventory of 1552 further included six surplices, six altar cloths, four cases, six corporasses, and a veil of old lawn—the Lenten Veil. In addition to the before-mentioned chalice and paten, the Commissioners delivered into the hands of the then churchwardens of Horseheath, John Bertlott and John Jorden, the blue bandekyn cope, the white damask cope, the purple silk vestment, six altar cloths and six surplices. These latter, however, were the only kind of gown permitted by the Prayer Book of 1552. The rest of the articles were left in the safe keeping of William Pettit, Lewis Flack, Reynold Buttell and John Webb, parishioners of Horseheath, who were held responsible for these goods, to be given up on demand. By this inventory we find there were in 1552 three bells in the tower, and a sanctus bell and two hand-bells. As nothing to the contrary is said of these bells, we presume that none of them were confiscated. This inventory is signed by five Cambridgeshire Commissioners, Henry Goderick, Richard Wilks, Thomas Rudstone, John Huddleston, and Thomas Bowles. These signatures are supplemented by that of Thomas Broderwyk, curate of Horseheath.

In pre-Reformation days, testamentary gifts to the Church were universal. Most frequently a sum of money was left for the High Altar, or for tithes, church repairs, masses for the souls of departed friends, or for some particular ornament or book, as in the case of John Pettit of Horseheath, who in 1512, in addition to a bequest to the Chapel of our Blessed Lady in Horseheath Church, left the sum of four marks for the purchase of a new grail[1]. This book and those included in the fourteenth century inventory are the only pre-Reformation service-books belonging to Horseheath Church of which we have any record. We regret that we have been unable to discover any information relating to much of pre-Reformation interest, such as an Eastern sepulchre, frescoes, chests, or coffers which must of necessity have been used for the safe keeping of the Church ornaments, vestments and valuables of various kinds. The locks and keys, massive or ornate according to the nature of such coffers, or even the lock and key which was used to secure the font, would be of great interest to us to-day.

It was under the sway of Puritanism, in the reign of Queen Elizabeth, that the churchyard cross at Horseheath comes to our notice. It probably stood on the south side of the chancel. It was of stone, and there were figures carved upon it, possibly the figure of the Saviour, or S. John and the Virgin. Its final destruction came about in 1580[2] owing to great reverence being made to it by certain of the parishioners as they passed by it to church, one aged woman being especially guilty of such reverence.

One of the most important features of the post-Reformation church furniture is the Communion Table which was substituted for the stone altar forbidden in 1550. The table now in the vestry, which was

---

[1] *Consistory Court of Ely*, E. 75.

[2] *Ely Consistory Court Book*, 1560–1580, f. 160.

discarded in 1883 for the present Communion Table or altar in the chancel, can scarcely be the original communion table, though it has few distinctive features by which a date may be assigned to it with any accuracy.

Reference has already been made to the Commission of 1643 in dealing with the Structure, when, under the superintendence of William Dowsing, the Church ornament then defaced appears to have been more in the nature of structural ornament than ornament of any kind in connection with the Church Furniture. However, at the time of William Dowsing's visit, there could have been little in Horseheath Church to offend the most staunch of reformers. It would be about the time of the Reformation that the wall paintings disappeared, and in their place the Commandments and verses of Scripture adorned the walls.

The Royal Arms, if not set up on the removal of the rood, were put up by compulsion at the Restoration in 1660, and were usually placed over the chancel screen. This is the position in which Cole found the arms of King George I in 1742[1]. On one side of the arms there was the date 1721, and on the other side G.R., and beneath the arms the motto "Fear God and honour the King." This motto remains to the parishioners of Horseheath to-day, but the date 1721 has been painted out and substituted by G.R. III. These arms were provided with a new frame in 1829 at a cost of one pound five shillings and sixpence. We remember that these Royal Arms formerly hung at the west end of the nave above

[1] *Addit. MS.* 5802, f. 5.

the gallery, and, when the tower arch was opened out in 1891, the arms were removed from the church, but found a place of refuge in the Rectory coach-house, where they remained until 1909, when they were restored and placed in their present position over the south door in the nave.

According to the Visitation returns of 1665[1], the furniture in Horseheath Church must then have been of the simplest character if the following small additions would make it perfect. It was ordered that the reading desk should be hung with cloth, and it was to have a fringe half a foot deep to match the cloth. A new linen cloth and a napkin were to be provided for the Communion Table. The chalice and paten were to be changed, and the new paten was to be made larger. This new chalice with its paten was in due time procured, and the date 1666 engraved upon it. At the present time, it is the most valuable piece of plate that the church possesses. It was also ordered at this Visitation of 1665 that the flagon should be gilded. This flagon has disappeared. A Book of Canons was to be procured and also a Book of Homilies, and Bishop Jewell's *Apology against Harding*.

An inventory of Horseheath Church goods made on the fourteenth day of June, 1692[2], included some of the items under notice in the Visitation of 1665. The first item in the 1692 inventory is the silver chalice with its paten. Then the flagon is entered. The next items mentioned are a green cloth carpet, a white linen cloth for the Communion Table, a Bible and two Books of Common Prayer, Bishop Jewell's

[1] Ely, *Parochial Visitation*, B. 3.   [2] Ely, *Terriers*, J. 1.

book against Harding, a surplice and hood, a cushion and carpet for the pulpit, a bier for the burial of the dead, a chest, a box for the church goods and writings. Four bells complete this list of goods. The inventory is signed by the rector, William Eedes, and Thomas Wakefield, churchwarden.

Seven years after the foregoing inventory was made, another bell was added to the peal of four. It is dated 1699, and has the names of the then churchwardens on it, Thomas Purkis and Thomas Rule. When the Rev. Thomas Percival was appointed to Horseheath Rectory in 1825, there were then, as now, only four bells. This rector made every effort to find out who it was who had sanctioned the reduction in the peal. No faculty had been granted for this purpose, but permission had been given to have the fourth and fifth bells recast, in order to make one bell of a tone suitable to the other three[1]. Whether this was done we are unable to say. In any case, one bell is dated MDCCCXXV. Yet if two bells were cast into one, we should have thought that the rector would not have been in ignorance of the fact, as appears by his correspondence with the Archdeacon[2]. Tradition says that one of the churchwardens sold a bell and absconded with the money. This bell dated 1825, whether recast or a new bell, in addition to the date, is inscribed with the bell-founder's name, T. Stafford, Cambridge, and W. Sanxter, J. Lawrence, C[hurch] W[ardens]. The Rev. J. J. Raven tells us[3]

[1] *Papers at Horseheath Rectory.*
[2] *Id.*
[3] *The Church Bells of Cambridgeshire*, p. 104.

that Thomas Stafford was a smith and bell-hanger
who lived near the Corn Exchange in Cambridge,
and that there are only two other bells made by him
in Cambridgeshire. One of these is at Trinity Hall,
and is dated 1804. The other is at Fen Drayton, and
is dated 1828. As to the other bells at Horseheath,
one records the fact that "Sir Giles Alington gave the
tenor" in 1606. This bell also bears the date 1700.
The same date is on the fourth bell without any other
inscription.

The two helmets, suspended on the north and
south walls in the chancel, are relics from the funerals
of the Bromley family. Under the helmet on
the north wall there formerly hung the sword and
buckler of John Bromley[1], who died in 1718. The
sword was in a scabbard of black velvet, and on the
buckler there were the Bromley arms. Over this
helmet there were four pennons charged with the
Bromley arms. There were also six pennons with
the Bromley arms over the window on the south
of the chancel, nearest the chancel arch[2]. These,
and the flags or pennons charged with the Alington
arms, which once adorned the chancel, some of them
over the Alington monument on the north of the
chancel, have all disappeared. But although Horseheath Church has lost much of interest in the way of
ornament, at the present time it possesses furniture
of considerable interest and beauty.

As already stated, the Communion plate includes
the elegant silver chalice, dated 1666, with its paten.
There is a fine silver flagon dated 1715; a silver

[1] *Addit. MS.* 5802, f. 5.　　[2] *Id.*

spoon, a glass cruet with silver stopper, and a large pewter plate or alms dish. An electro-plated paten must be mentioned with an apology.

There are a three-stepped brass cross on the altar, two large brass vases, two smaller brass vases, and a brass bookstand. There is a brass ewer for the font, which we believe was purchased by the Horseheath school children.

A modern oak chest has recently been put in the chancel for the altar frontals, of which there are five :

1. Green silk damask with an embroidered cross in gold thread in the centre, with gold velvet orpheries. These and the frontals are fringed with green wool and gold silk.

2. Purple cloth with I.H.S. in the centre, encircled by a crown of thorns of plaited white braid.

3. White and gold tapestry, with white and gold fringe.

4. Red velvet embroidered with a conventional border finished with a gold, red, white and blue fringe.

5. Red velvet with a handsomely embroidered centre ornament of conventional roses, fleur-de-lis and pomegranates, and I.H.S. in silver thread worked upon a cross of blue silk in the centre. The panels on either side are embroidered with similar conventional designs in a variety of colours. This frontal is finished with a gold, red, blue and black fringe.

The upper frontals include :

1. Green plush edged with gold braid.

2. Purple cloth panelled with strips of white braid.

3. White and gold damask.

4. Red cloth with strips of red embroidery.

Rear-Altar Cloths:

1. Gold and white embroidery, which came from the street called Straight, Jerusalem, mentioned in Acts xii. 11.

2. Red velvet and gold braid.

Frontlets:

1. Red velvet edged with a band of red and white embroidery, fringed with red, green, white and gold.

2. Purple cloth, with red, purple and white silk fringe.

3. Red velvet, with the words "Holy, Holy, Holy" embroidered in gold and outlined with black silk and gold thread, with two roses on either side of the centre "Holy" embroidered in red and white silk, outlined with black silk and gold thread. The fringe is red and gold silk.

Altar Cloths:

1. Fine linen damask fringed.

2. Embroidered linen.

Fair Linen Cloth, one. Embroidered.

Corporal, one. Embroidered linen.

Lace Chalice Veils, two.

Chalice Veils:

1. White silk damask with an embroidered cross in pink silk, with a border of gold thread finished with a white silk cord.

2. Green silk edged with a band of green and gold embroidery.

3. Purple silk edged with a band of purple and white embroidery.

4. Red silk edged with red and gold.

Purificators. Several.

Offertory Bags:

1. Two bags and one plate-cover in red velvet, embroidered with gold.

2. A similar set of purple velvet embroidered with white silk, finished with a white silk cord.

Lectern Cloths:

1. White silk damask, with a rose embroidered in gold silk, fringed with white silk.

2. Green silk damask with an embroidered rose of conventional design, fringed with green wool and gold silk.

3. Embossed gold velvet fringed with gold silk.

Pulpit Cloths:

1. Embossed gold velvet fringed with gold silk.

2. Green silk damask with a conventional rose embroidered in the centre, fringed with green silk and gold wool.

Book-Markers:

1. A set of four in red silk, finished with gold silk fringe.

2. Three of purple silk, with white silk fringe.

3. Three of white silk, with gold silk fringe.

4. Four of green silk, with green and gold fringe.

Palls, one. White, with a yellow cross upon it.

Flags, one. S. George.

The blue tapestry curtain which serves as a screen for the organist must not pass without notice, it being a piece of material used in Westminster Abbey at the Coronation of King Edward the Seventh, and was especially designed for that occasion.

There is no parish chest in Horseheath Church, but in the eighteenth century there appear to have been two. One in the vestry, and the other in the chancel[1].

The oak lectern has a small plate inscribed "Presented by Jane Theophilis Mary Nunn, November 21st, 1883." The well-preserved Oxford Bible on this lectern was printed at the Theatre in 1685. It has a printed label on the cover, which reads: "Parish of Horseheath, 1846, Wm. Parker, John Webb, Church-wardens." Possibly it was rebound at this date.

Owing to the destruction of the early Horseheath churchwardens' accounts and other parish records, much of interest is lost to us. The parish register, however, is fairly complete from the year 1558.

The present organ, which used to stand in the gallery at the west end of the nave, was bought second-hand from a church in Cambridge, about the year 1876. There were two barrels in the old organ, and George Poulter was the last man who had the honour of turning the handle to provide music for an appreciative audience, all of whom, from the school children in the chancel to the adult congregation in the square pews, or in the long pews facing or endways to the pulpit, stood, and turned their faces to the gallery to join in the singing.

With reference to the church clock, a small brass plate in the tower records that

"The Clock in this Tower
was erected by subscription to
Commemorate 60 years reign of
Good Queen Victoria
1837–1897
C. A. Borrer, Rector
A. Kent, W. Hymus, Churchwardens."

[1] *Addit. MS.* 5802, f. 5.

CHAPTER III

THE MONUMENTS

THERE are no incised slabs in Horseheath Church. The earliest memorial in the church is an exceptionally fine fourteenth century brass which we have reason to believe commemorates William de Audley, who died in the year 1365[1]. This brass has been attributed by various writers to Sir John de Argentine of Halesworth, Suffolk, who died in 1382[2]. Incidentally we may mention, that this gentleman's widow Margaret survived him one year, and in her will[3] she directed that she should be buried in S. Mary's Church, Halesworth, and the probability is that Sir John de Argentine had previously been buried there. The whole of the inscription round the fourteenth century brass is now missing, but when Cole visited Horseheath Church in 1742, on the dexter side of the brass there remained the following words in black letter, " De Novemb L'an de l'Incarnacion..."[4] from which we may infer that the man whom the brass commemorates died in the month of November. On searching the *Inquisitiones Post Mortem* of persons connected with Horseheath

---

[1] *Inquisitiones Post Mortem*, 39 Edw. III, 1st Nos. 1.
[2] *Baker's MS.* xvi. f. 234.   [3] *Addit. MS.* 19, 115, f. 130.
[4] *Addit. MS.* 5802.

during the last half of the fourteenth century—
obviously the period of the brass—we find that the
only manorial holder of Horseheath who died in the
month of November, about that time, was William de
Audley, whose death occurred on the eleventh of
November, 1365. Therefore, in the absence of re-
butting evidence, it is to William de Audley we
attribute this brass, and not to a member of the
Argentine family, whose connection with Horseheath
parish did not begin till a later date, when William,
and his brother Robert Alington of Horseheath,
married Elizabeth and Joan, the Argentine co-heiresses,
probably great grand-daughters of the Sir John de
Argentine above mentioned[1]. The brass in question—
in a Purbeck marble matrix—now lies on the chancel
floor within the altar rails. It is a particularly fine
example of the Carmail period, so called from the
tippet of mail which covers the neck and shoulders.
The pointed steel cap, the mailshirt just showing
below the jupon and at the armpits, the arm defences,
steel gauntlets, thigh armour, jambs, rowel spurs, the
particularly long sword, and the remaining portion of
the canopy are all interesting features of this brass.
Originally there were two angels supporting the family
arms. The armour clad figure measures four feet three
and a half inches. This is the only brass[2] in Horseheath Church that belongs to the fourteenth century.

The earliest monumental slab of the fifteenth
century is that which commemorates one of the

[1] Harleian Society's *Visitation of Cambridge*, p. 15.
[2] Illustrated in the Rev. H. W. Macklin's *Monumental Brasses*,
p. 58.

Argentine co-heiresses before mentioned, Joan, the wife of Robert Alington, who died in 1429, before she was eighteen years of age. This slab lies on the chancel floor by the north wall, and is now covered by the choir seats. The brass figure of the lady is missing as well as the inscription plate at the foot. The inscription however has been recorded as follows :— " Hic jacet Joañ Alyngton soror et una heredū Johīs Argenteyn filii Johīs filii Willm̄ Argentyne Militis que obiit XVᵒ die Maii MᵒCCCCXXIX¹."

The Purbeck marble matrix at the entrance of the chancel has lost both of its brass figures. The knight measured one foot nine inches and the lady one foot seven inches. These were the figures of William Alington and his wife Elizabeth², the other Argentine co-heiress. From the matrix we see that this lady, who died in 1445, wore the horned headdress of fifteenth century fashion. Her husband is represented with a helmet, his sword on the left, and a dagger on his right, with a dog at his feet. The two shields which bore the Alington arms quartered with Argentine, as well as the inscription plate, are now missing, but in 1695 the shields were intact.

An interesting Alington inscription from a brass plate on a slab in Horseheath Church is recorded in a marginal note in *The Pedigree of the Alington family copied from the original in the possession of George Marmaduke Alington, Esquire, of Swinhope House, Co. Lincs., also their descent through heirs general from the Ancient family of Argentine,*

¹ *Harleian MS.* 6821, f. 50.
² *Id.*

Lords of Wymondley in Hertfordshire 1867[1]. The inscription is given as follows:—"William Alington Armiger, Thesaurarius Henrici quarti in Hibernia Ac etiam Henrici quinti in Normandie obiit 19. Oct. 1446. King Henry VI. 24. Et Joanna uxor ejus obiit 27 Feb. 1445." This William Alington, Treasurer of Ireland, and his wife Joan were the mother and father of the William and Robert Alington who married the Argentine co-heiresses. It has occurred to us that the above inscription may be from the plate missing from the large Purbeck marble slab

in the nave, from which neither Cole in 1742, nor King in 1695, copied any inscription. When the workmen were taking up the old brick floor in 1891, they came in contact with a coffin near this matrix, the earth above was disturbed as little as possible, and no inscription, if any on the coffin, was copied. On the other hand, the plate bearing the above inscription may have become detached from the altar tomb of which we here give a conjectural drawing[2].

[1] Kindly lent to the author by Mrs Royds of Oaklands, Fenstanton, Cambridgeshire.

[2] See p. 7.

The next memorial in Horseheath Church, in chronological order, is a brass inscription plate which also belongs to the Alington family. It measures 6½ inches by 1 foot 2½ inches. The original matrix for this brass has been missing for at least three hundred years. For some years it lay detached in the vestry. It is inscribed in black letter "Nobilis ecce pia jacet hic formosa Maria | Que laurence Cheyne prosilit e gene'e | uxor et Alington quōdm̄ fuit illa Johīs | Armigerii: sup est marmoris ecce lapis | Post mundi tenebras cōcede de⁹ bone lucem | Qua vivat tecū, qui sine fine manes." Dr Basset, who was rector of Horseheath from 1709 to 1732, translated this inscription for Lady Howe, a descendant of Mary Alington who died in 1473, as follows :—

"Lo here ye noble Mary lyes, as good and fair as any,
  Springing from ye race and ancient stock of Squire Hight,
    Laurence Cheyne
  Wife heretofore she was unto John Alington, Esquire
  And now below a marble stone lyes or very nigh her.
  After this worldly darkness past, grant that great God she may
  Forever live with Thee, who are forever and for aye[1]."

It was in 1883, chiefly through the instigation of Mr F. Wm. Alington that this inscription plate was placed on the south wall of the chancel, together with an additional plate in a white marble matrix. The second inscription records that "This ancient brass in memory of Mary wife of John Alington | (Sheriff of Cambs. 1. Ed. IV.) was placed for safe keeping | near the tomb of her grandson by their descendants at the | restoration of this chancel A.D. 1883."

[1] *Addit. MS.* 5802.

Within the altar rails to the south of the chancel
there is a brass to the memory of Robert Alington
who died in 1552. The brass figure measures 2 feet
6 inches by 11½ inches. Unfortunately the head is
missing from the figure. A shield on the dexter
side—the sinister corner of which is missing—bears
the four quarterings of Alington: 1. sable, a bend
engrailed between six billets, argent. 2. Argentine,
gules, three covered cups, argent. 3. Fitz-Tec, azure,
five martlets, two, two and one, or, a canton ermine.
4. Gardener, per fesse argent and sable, a pale counter
charged between three griffons' heads, erased. Impaling the arms, gules, a crescent between three conies
couchant, argent, a bordure engrailed, sable, for
Coningsby, Robert Alington having married Margaret,
the daughter of William Coningsby. The shield on
the sinister side bears the arms of Alington, Argentine,
Fitz-Tec, and Gardener, over all a label of three
points, or. High up on the south wall of the nave
there is a small stone shield now covered with whitewash, though the carving is distinct; the tinctures
are recorded by Cole who described the shield as
bearing the Gardener arms, impaling, argent, a
chevron between three griffons' heads, or. Cole
however considered that the blazoning had been
incorrectly done when the church was repainted. He
says that in the next window—the most easterly
window on the south—the same arms were blazoned
baron and femme, first Gardener, impaling, sable,
a chevron between three griffons' heads, argent, for
Cotton.

In accordance with the will of Sir Giles Alington,

dated 1579[1], the fine monument on the south side of the chancel was erected in 1586 (see illustration). Sir Giles Alington in his will directs that he should be buried without superfluous pomp on the south side of the chancel, where his second wife Alice Middleton was buried. The monument was to be erected within a year after Sir Giles's death, and on it was to be inscribed who he was, whom he married, the number of his children, and who was his heir. He further directed that a monument should be put up over his father's grave with a similar inscription. This is somewhat strange, since Sir Giles Alington's father expressed a wish in his will, dated 1522[2], that he should be buried in the Priory at Wymondley which was founded by his ancestors. If his wish was carried out, probably his remains were removed to Horseheath at the dissolution of that Priory. The monument is of clunch. Formerly there was an ornate canopy at the back of it with shields with armorial bearings on it, and two small figures on either side. That portion now standing on the monument is the top of the canopy, which originally blocked the whole of the window behind. The shield on this remaining part of the canopy bears the quarterings of Alington, Argentine, Fitz-Tec and Alington, above which is the Alington crest, a talbot passant, proper, ermine. There are two shields below, at the back of this monument, that on the dexter has the same four quarterings as above, impaling, per fesse argent and sable, a pale counter charged between three griffons' heads erased of the second for Gardener.

---

[1] P. P. C. *Windsor*, f. 492.   [2] P. P. C. *Porch*, f. 14.

Alington Monument, 1586.

The sinister shield bears the arms of Alington, Argentine, Fitz-Tec and Alington.

On a frieze round the monument there are four shields at the north end, the arms however on these shields are completely defaced. The leaded lettering of the inscription on the frieze is particularly good, and reads as follows:—" Here under lyeth buryed, Sir Gyles Alington, Knight, who died, 25 Aprilis, An. 1522. He maryed Marye, the only daughter and heire, of Sir Richard Gardener, Knighte, and by her had issue, Gyles, George, William, John, Anthonie, Roberte, Richarde, Awdrye, Joanne and Marye." That part of the monument upon which the upper figure rests is covered with lead. On this there are three inscriptions, that at the side refers to Sir Giles Alington under whose will the monument was erected:—" Sir Gyles Knight Sonne and Heyre of Sir Gyles Alington Knight died 20 Augustii Ano. 1586, and in the year of his age 86. He first married Ursula, Daughter of Sir Robert Drury, Knighte, and by her had issue, Robert. Secondly, he married Alice, Daughter and Heyre of John Middleton, Esquire, before wife of Thomas Elrington, Esquire, and by her had issue Thomas, Richard, William, Phillip, Ann, Frances, Elizabeth, Jane, and Margaret, and thirdly he married Margaret daughter of John Talkakerne Esquire, before wife of Thomas Argall Esquire and by her had no issue." The inscription at the foot is to Robert Alington, whose monumental brass has already been mentioned. " Robert Alington Esquire, sonne and heyre apparent of Sir Gyles Alington Knight died 22 Maii, Ano. 1552. He married Margaret daughter of William Coniesbye, one of the judges of the law, and by her had issue, John, Giles, James, George, Alice, Ann, Margaret, Elizabeth, Frances, and Beatrice." The following inscription is at the head:— "Gyles Alington, Esquire, son and heyre of Robert Alington Esquire and Heyre apparent unto Sir Gyles Alyngton Knight died 25° November Ano. 1572. He married Margaret daughter of Sir John Spencer, Knight, and by her had issue, Gyles, John, Margaret, which Gyles last named being great grandchild unto the said Sir Gyles was also at his decease his next heyre." The present somewhat sombre appearance of this monument must contrast strangely with the display of heraldry, the ornamental canopy, and the painted effigies, that it possessed when first erected.

There are no less than five sixteenth century monumental brasses missing from Horseheath Church which Blomefield placed on record when he visited the church on the eighth of April, 1726. When Cole visited the church in 1747 he sketched these brasses[1]. The earliest of these five brasses was dated 1504[2]. On it was the figure of a man and a plate with an inscription, and, although inscribed as follows, was not deleted by Dowsing:—"Orate pro Animabus Johannis | Kent, Katherine et Agnetis uxorum | ejus qui prefatus Johannes obiit | xviij Die Mens. Nov. A° Dm. M°CCCCC°IV | quorum animabus propicietur Deus."

Between the north and south doors of the nave, there was a brass with the figure of a man in a long

---

[1] *Addit. MS.* 5805.
[2] *Transactions of the Monumental Brass Society*, Vol. v, Pt. 1, p. 11.

furred gown, with a gipciere in front. The inscription
plate bore the words "Orate pro anima Johannis |
Theilgar qui obiit ult. die Maii A° Dni MCCCCCviij."
To the left of this brass there was a slab which had
a small figure of a man upon it. The inscription plate
at the foot was inscribed "Hic Jacet Wills Colyn
geñosus | qñdm̄. uñ justīc Dñi Reg. ad Pacem | in
Cont. Cant. cōservand q'obiit 11 die | April A° Dñi
MCCCCCXXI cujus aīe ꝑpicietur Deus."

Cole found in a chest in the chancel part of an
inscription plate which had become detached from its
matrix below the figure of a woman, on which was in-
scribed, "Hic jacet Willm̄ Collyn qui | obiit X° die
Dcmb A° Dñi M° CCCCCVII cuᵞ aīe ꝑpicieꝶ Deus."
The other missing sixteenth century slab was by the
south entrance of the nave and was designed for the
figure of a man. It was inscribed "Hic jacet Em.
Jaxley qui ob[iit] | XXI die Decemb. A° Dni
MCCC[CC]xliij cuᵞ aīe ꝑpicietur De[us]."

We now pass on to the seventeenth century
monuments, the earliest being the handsome alabaster
monument on the north side of the chancel, within
the altar rails. It was erected in 1613, when the
church appears to have been in an extremely dilapidated
condition, by Sir Giles Alington, the great-grandson
and heir of Sir Giles Alington who made provision in
his will for the erection of the monument on the south
side of the chancel. The monument on the north was
erected in memory of Lady Dorothy, daughter of the
Earl of Exeter, Sir Giles Alington's first wife (see
frontispiece). The whole of the monument was evidently painted and gilded. A considerable portion of

the colouring is shown in the water colour drawing of this monument in the Relhan Collection[1]. Lady Dorothy is represented wearing a black dress. The recumbent effigies of Sir Giles in armour and Lady Dorothy on this monument are both well preserved. We learn from Cole that formerly the Cecil crest was at Lady Dorothy's feet, a garb, or, between two lions, rampant, the dexter argent, the sinister azure. It is interesting to be able to record that on comparing the engraving of Sir Giles Alington in Lodge's *Lives of the Caesars*, from a portrait by Cornelius Janssen, that the effigy on this monument presents a particularly good likeness. There are the figures of six children at the front of this monument in a kneeling position. Originally there were three other children at the head, these being in clunch were so dilapidated in 1829, that they were removed. There was also a child, holding a death's head in his hands, at the foot of the monument. The monument was formerly surmounted by a death's head, with gilded wings, and there were obelisks in white marble on either side. The bases for these still remain. The centre shield at the top of the monument bears the quarterings of Alington, Argentine, Fitz-Tec, Gardener, already described, and Middleton, which arms Sir Giles was not entitled to bear, since he was descended from Ursula Drury, his grandfather's first wife, and not Alice Middleton, who was his grandfather's second wife. Over the helmet, above this shield, there is the Alington crest, a talbot passant, proper, ermine. A shield on the centre of the frieze bears the arms of Alington, Argentine, Fitz-Tec, Gardener, Middleton.

[1] The Library of the Cambridge Antiquarian Society.

Argent, fetty, sable, with a canton of the last, and Alington, impaling Cecil. Barry of ten, argent and azure, over all six escutcheons, three, two and one, sable, each charged with a lion rampant, of the first. On the dexter side of the centre shield, there is a shield with the six quarterings of 1. Cecil. 2. Winston, partly per pale, azure and gules, a lion rampant, argent, holding a tree uprooted, proper. 3. Carlyon, sable, a plate between three towers, argent. 4. (?) Heckington, argent, on a bend, cotised, gules, three roses, or. 5. Walcot, argent, a chevron between three chess rooks ermine. 6. Cecil.

The inscription on this monument in gilt lettering is as follows :—" Here resteth in assured Hope to rise in Christ Sir Giles Alington of Horseheath, Knight, accompanied | with Lady Dorothy, his wife, Daughter of Thomas | Earle of Exeter, Baron Burghley, and who made him a joyfull Father of tenne Children, viz. | (Elizabeth, Thomas, Giles, James, Dorothy, Susan, Anne, Catherine, William and Mary) | ended this transitory life the 10th of November | 1613, to whose dear memory her sorrowfull Husband mindful | of his own mortality erected this monument." It was William, the youngest son, who married Elizabeth Tollmarsh, who became his father's heir.

During the restoration of the chancel in 1829 three brass inscription plates were discovered near leaden coffins under the chancel floor that belonged to members of the Alington family. The inscriptions were respectively[1] :—1. " Here lieth the body of the Right Honourable Katherine Lady Alington, wife

[1] *Coll. Topo. et Gen.* Vol. III. p. 33.

to the Right Honourable William Lord Alington of Horseheath, Cambridgeshire, and second daughter to the Right Honourable The Countess of Chesterfield, who departed this life the 19th day of November 1662, there with child, of her first child, and being a daughter, that is interred in the same coffin with her." This lady was buried on the fourth of December 1662. 2. "The Body of ye Honble William Alington, son and heir to the Right Honble William Lord Alington by his Lady Juliana daughter to the Right Honble Baptist Viscount Camden. He died ye 3rd day of September 1677, aged 13 days." 3. "The body of the Right Honble Juliana Lady Alington, daughter of the Right Honble Baptist Viscount Camden 2nd wife of the Right Honble William Lord Alington by whom he had issue Juliana now living and William deceased." She died the 14th day of September, 1667, aged 22 years.

The two ladies here mentioned were the first and second wives of William, Lord Alington, grandson of Sir Giles Alington, who erected the Alington monument on the north of the chancel; his third wife, Diana Russell, survived her husband.

There is a seventeenth century mural tablet on the middle of the chancel north wall, of clunch and grey marble. On either side of the centre foliated ornament at the top, there were originally two large bibles, and the whole of the tablet was decorated with gilt. This tablet was put up at the cost of ten pounds in accordance with the instructions expressed by Thomas Wakefield, rector of Horseheath, in his will[1] dated the eighth of November 1626. The tablet is inscribed :—

[1] *Cons. Court of Ely, Bury,* f. 81.

"Depositū Thomæ Wakefield 37 Annos Eccłiae |
hujus Rectoris nec non Judithae uxoris | ejus quibus
parentavit Filius Thomas, | qui Patri in hac Rectoria
successit | An° Dni 1627."

To pass on to the eighteenth century memorials,
there is, on the north wall of the chancel, a tablet in
memory of another rector of Horseheath. This mural
tablet is of alabaster and grey marble. On the entablature above the inscription, there are three urns,
those on either side have flames coming out of them.
Cherubim support the tablet which bears the following
inscription :—"Here under interred lyeth the Body
of William Eedes...late of this Parish of Horseheath
who departed this life the 23rd day of April Anno
Dom. 1709 aged 68."

A white marble memorial tablet, on the south wall
of the chancel, commemorates four members of the
Bromley family. This family succeeded the Alingtons
as lords of the manor of Horseheath about the year
1687. In dealing with the structure of Horseheath
Church we have already mentioned the Bromley
mortuary chapel, but it will be interesting here to
record the inscriptions[1] copied from the plates on the
four coffins, covered in black velvet, that Cole found
in this chapel when he visited the church. After the
destruction of the chapel in 1828 the coffins were
re-interred under the chancel floor. A stone is placed
over the entrance of the vault (No. 7 on plan), inscribed, "The Bromleys." The coffin on the south
next the chancel wall in the mortuary chapel, Cole
says, bore the Bromley arms over a plate inscribed :—

[1] *Addit. MS.* 5808, f. 169.

"The Body of the Hon. John Bromley, Esq. | who
departed this life Octob. 17. | 1707 in the 56 year of
his age." Another coffin bore a plate inscribed :—
" Mrs Dorothy Bromley | died July ye 14th 1709 |
aged 60 years." A very large coffin bore the Bromley
arms and an inscription plate inscribed :—" John
Bromley, Esq. died | Octob. 20, 1718 in ye 36 | year
of his age." On the fourth coffin there was no
inscription plate at all. The mural tablet on the
south wall of the chancel before mentioned is to the
memory of these four members of the Bromley family.
On a medallion at the top there are the Bromley arms.
Quarterly per fesse, dancetté, gules and or, with an
escutcheon of pretence over it, argent, a griffon
rampant, vert. Above these arms is the Bromley
crest, a demi lion, sable, issuing from a ducal coronet,
or, holding a flag, or, with a lion passant, gules. We
believe the tincture of this flag should be gules, with
a lion passant, or. The inscription on the tablet is as
follows :—" In a vault beneath the north window of
this chancel are deposited the remains of | the
Hon^able | John Bromley, | one of the Supreme Council
of Barbados | And M.P. for the county of Cambridge |
He died 17th October 1707 aged 55, | and his wife
Dorothy, daughter of Thomas White | of Fittleford
in the County of Dorset, Esqre. | She died 14th
July 1709 aged 60 | Also of their two sons John
and William. | William second son died unmarried
26 November 1729 aged 40. | John Bromley Esqre
eldest son | died M.P. for this County 20 Oct. 1718
aged 36. | Having married Mercy, daughter and
heiress | of William Bromley of Holt Castle | in the

county of Worcestershire, Esqre | who died in Child bed 5 August 1705 aged 17 | of a son Henry created in 1741 Lord Montfort, Baron of Horseheath in the county of Cambridge."

On the chancel floor there is a stone slab to the memory of Philip Bearcroft, who was appointed to Horseheath rectory in 1758. Except for the following words the inscription is defaced. " Phillippis Bearcroft ...s Eccle......Rector | ...1 Feb. A.D. 1776 | E...45."

On the south wall of the chancel there is a small white marble tablet in memory of John Maule, Philip Bearcroft's successor. It is inscribed " M.S. | of | The Rev. John Maule | for 47 years Rector of this Parish | He died at Bath the 20th of January 1825 | in the 77th year of his age | and was buried in St James Church | in that City. He was lineally descended | from the noble and ancient family | of Panmure in Scotland."

In the nave there are four nineteenth century mural tablets in memory to members of the Batson family. This family acquired the manor of Horseheath from the Bromleys in 1783. Two of these tablets are at the east end of the nave on the dexter side of the chancel arch. They are of white marble, and are respectively inscribed :—" Sacred to the memory of Stanlake Batson | of Horseheath Lodge | in this Parish, | who died July 11. 1857 | in the 84th year of his age." And " Sacred to the memory of | Isabella Batson | the beloved wife of Stanlake Batson | of | Horseheath Lodge | in this Parish | and daughter of the late George Poyntz Ricketts Esquire | Governor of Barbados | She died

December 7th 1845 | aged 63 years." The mural brass on the south wall of the nave has the Batson crest— a bat's wing, erect, argent—above the inscription :— "Sacred to the memory of Stanlake Ricketts Batson | of Horseheath | Born 11th November 1819 | Died 13th June 1871, | and of Gertrude Julianna Louise Batson his wife | Born 30th June 1831. | Died 16th February 1874."

A small brass tablet on the north wall is in memory of the second son of the above-named Stanlake Ricketts Batson. This brass also has the Batson crest. It is inscribed, "Sacred to the memory of | Montague Edward Batson | Son of Stanlake Ricketts Batson | of Horseheath, | Born 15th Septr. 1865. Died 26th May 1881." This youth died at Stone Vicarage, Buckinghamshire, and was buried in the churchyard there, where a cross has been erected to his memory.

Beneath the small Batson brass on the north wall, there is a small white marble tablet which has the following inscription :—"Erected by the Parishioners | to the memory of | Emma Hall, | for many years a faithful and respected teacher | in the Horseheath schools. | She fed them with a faithful | and true heart." This school teacher died on the twenty-third of April 1902. The date has been omitted on the tablet erected to her memory in the church.

CHAPTER IV

THE ADVOWSON

In the absence of evidence to the contrary, there is every reason to believe that Horseheath Church owes its foundation to the de Vere family, and that from earliest times the Advowson of the Church was owned by that family, so closely connected with the neighbourhood. In 1086 Aubrey de Vere, ancestor of the Earls of Oxford, who married Beatrice, sister of William the Conqueror, owned an estate at Horseheath amongst the vast possessions granted to him by the Conqueror. These possessions were of such magnitude that it seems unlikely that their owner could have been personally acquainted with all of them. Castle Camps, only about two miles from Horseheath, was also granted to Aubrey de Vere, and till about the year 1580 the family had a residence in that parish. It was probably Aubrey de Vere's son or grandson, both of whom were named Aubrey, who in King Stephen's reign built the castle at Hedingham, Essex, about seventeen miles from Horseheath, and apparently the chief residence of the de Vere family. We believe that certain rights and services due from the de Veres' manorial tenants in Horseheath, and subsequently the advowson of Horseheath, descended in a direct line from Aubrey de Vere to the successive Earls of

Oxford, though we have not been able to discover a precise date of any presentation prior to that made by John de Vere, seventh Earl of Oxford, in 1347[1]. This Earl, and his Countess Elizabeth, had previously, in 1342, leased the advowson of Horseheath Church with manors in Cambridgeshire, Suffolk and Berkshire for a short period to Richard de Stock, cleric, and John Fermer[2]. Between the years 1360 and 1371[3] Aubrey de Vere had let the advowson to Elizabeth, widow of Aubrey Luterall, Kt. Afterwards the advowson passed to Elizabeth, Countess of Oxford. This Countess made a presentation in 1386[4], and owned the advowson at the time of her death in 1395[5].

When the next vacancy occurred the advowson was, on the thirty-first of October, 1395, in the hands of Aubrey de Vere[6], the tenth Earl of Oxford, and son of the seventh Earl. The tenth Earl died in 1399[7], the advowson of Horseheath Church then passed to his son Richard, the eleventh Earl. This Earl died in 1416 at the age of thirty-eight years[8], when his son John, the twelfth Earl, was only two years old. In 1455[9] the advowson was in the hands of this Earl, who, on account of his disloyalty to King Edward IV, was beheaded in 1461. His

---

[1] *Bp de Insula's Register*, f. 9 b.
[2] *Feet of Fines*, 16/17 Edw. III, No. 314.
[3] Dr W. M. Palmer, *Feet of Fines for Cambridgeshire*, p. 12.
[4] *Bp Arundel's Reg.* f. 58 b.
[5] *Inq. Post Mortem*, 19 Ric. II, No. 74.
[6] *Bp Fordham's Register*, f. 49.
[7] *Inq. Post Mortem*, 1 Hen IV, No. 52, memb. 4.
[8] *Inq. Post Mortem*, 4 Hen. V, No. 53.
[9] *Bp Gray's Register*, f. 10.

possessions were granted by letters patent[1] to Richard, Duke of Gloucester. Consequently we find that when the next presentation was made in 1474, the advowson belonged to the Duke of Gloucester[2]. The next presentation was made in 1500, when the conflicting Wars of the Roses were at an end, and the de Vere possessions had been restored to John de Vere, the thirteenth Earl, and son of the supporter of the Lancastrian cause. The advowson next passed to the fourteenth Earl, also named John, who succeeded his uncle in 1512[3] when thirteen years of age. He resided at Castle Camps, and, although almost an imbecile, was married at the age of fourteen to Anne, second daughter of the Duke of Norfolk. According to letters concerning him[4], written by his wife to her father and Wolsey, he was apparently quite incapable of looking after his affairs, and his advisors appear to have been eminently unsatisfactory. Therefore, it may have been through certain legal mismanagement, that difficulties arose concerning the right of presentation in the year 1556[5], when there was a dispute as to who was the right owner of the Horseheath advowson. The fourteenth Earl died without children in 1526 and was succeeded by his cousin John, the fifteenth Earl, who died in 1538. He was succeeded by his son John, the sixteenth Earl, who it appears on the

[1] *Patent Roll*, 1462, memb. 5.
[2] *Bp Gray's Register*, f. 91 b.
[3] *Inq. Post Mortem*, 5 Hen. VIII, No. 123.
[4] Brit. Mus. *Hargrave MS.* No. 227, f. 237.
[5] *Baker MS.* xxviii, f. 295.

death of William Masterson, rector of Horseheath in 1556, claimed the Horseheath advowson for that turn, and presented Thomas White. At the same time the dowager Countess Doageria claimed the advowson in right of her dowry, and presented Richard Chapman. Hence doubt arose as to who was the legal owner of the advowson. It was arranged that twelve clerics, and twelve laymen with Thomas White, Richard Chapman, the Earl and the dowager Countess should appear in Horseheath Church on Monday, the fifth of April, 1556[1], to investigate the matter with such evidence, letters and muniments as they had at their disposal relating to the case. The questions to be answered were as follows. Was the parish church of Horseheath vacant, and how? How long had the living been vacant, and when did the vacancy begin? Who was last presented? Who ought to present? What was the manner of life, and the amount of learning of Thomas White and Richard Chapman respectively? The result of these enquiries ended in favour of the Earl's presentation to Thomas White in 1557. This was the last presentation made to the Horseheath living by the de Vere family. Edward de Vere, the seventeenth Earl of Oxford, son of John, the sixteenth Earl, was reckless and practically ruined the family fortune. Although the actual owner of the Horseheath advowson, he had let the turn of presentation, when a vacancy occurred in 1589, to Philip Mynott, whose executors, Robert Bentley and Richard Worlich *alias* Mynott, presented Thomas Wakefield for that turn[2]. This rector

---

[1] *Baker MS.* xxviii, f. 295.   [2] *Lambeth Register*, f. 324 a.

apparently rented the advowson in order that his son might succeed him at Horseheath, and made provision to this effect in his will[1], dated the eighth day of November, 1626, which is here abstracted :—

"I Thomas Wakefield of Horseheath, Clerk...... bequeath......my body to be buried in the chancel of Horseheath Church. I give ten pounds for a monument for a memorial of me in the middle part of the North Wall of the said Chancel.... I give and bequeath unto the town of Horseheath forever fifty pounds of lawful money of England for a town stack for ye yearly relief of the poor to be given them at two times in the year, that is, at the Nativity of our Lord God, and at Easter. And further my will is that ye Churchwardens for the time being shall have the said fifty pounds paid them within one year next after my decease, and for to remain to the Churchwardens, they giving severally to the Minister of the said town for performance of this my will. And further my will is that it shall be lawful for the Churchwardens at any time hereafter to bestow the said fifty pounds in some lands to the use abovesaid, the which I would have done with as much speed as they can. To my kinsman William George the advowson of the Church and parsonage of Horseheath abovesaid upon this condition, that he shall freely give it unto my son Thomas Wakefield after my decease. To Judith, wife of William George six pounds yearly, to be paid quarterly to begin the day of my death. My debtors to pay in the money they owe me within six months after my death. To every

[1] *Cons. Court of Ely, Bury*, f. 81.

of my servants with me at the time of my death ten shillings each more than their wages.... I will that if my son Thomas aforesaid die without issue I give all my free houses and lands with appurtenances unto Thomas and John Wakefield, sons of my brother John Wakefield, and to their heirs on condition they pay six score pounds to all the children of my three sisters Katherine, Margerie, and Barbara within three years next after the death of my said son Thomas, for dying without issue. I give to my said son Thomas all my other goods whatsoever whom I make my sole executor. I ordain William George to be the supervisor of this my last will, to whom I bequeath the sum of four pounds for his paines."

This will was proved on the sixteenth of December, 1626, and, only two days later, we find that Thomas Wakefield's son Thomas was duly presented[1] to Horseheath Rectory by William George, as requested by the testator. It was in this same year 1626, that Henry, the eighteenth Earl of Oxford, died. He was succeeded by Robert, the nineteenth Earl, who died in 1632, and from a certificate of his estate dated 1634[2] we find that the assessed value of the advowson of Horseheath Church was three pounds per annum. This nineteenth Earl was succeeded by his son Aubrey, the twentieth and last Earl of Oxford. But the turn vacant in 1668, and all subsequent vacancies, have been filled by the Governors of Charterhouse.

Charterhouse was founded as a Hospital by Thomas Sutton in 1611, and, under the Charter and

[1] *Horseheath Parish Register.*　　　　[2] *Addit. MS.* 5838, f. 86 a.

Bargain of Sale of 1611, he gave the Governors all his advowsons in Cambridgeshire and other counties. Precisely how and when the Horseheath advowson was obtained for Charterhouse we regret we have not been able to discover. It was in the hands of the Governors in 1624[1]. It was they who granted the Rev. Thomas Wakefield, senior[1], the right of presentation, since when, the succeeding presentations have been made by the Governors. Therefore it is strange that the advowson should be valued in the estate of Robert, Earl of Oxford, after his death in 1632. There is a note against the Order appointing Mr Bassett in 1709 as follows:—"Mem. y[t] one Mr Parker of Swaffham Bulbeck pretended to ye R[t] of Patronage etc., and also the Duke of St Albans as claiming under the Earl of Oxford, but both desisted after the Governors' clerk was instituted by the Bishop[1]."

[1] Information kindly given by H. S. Wright, Esq., 'Registrar' of Charterhouse.

CHAPTER V

THE VALUATION

From the assessment of ecclesiastical property in England in 1256 for the purpose of granting King Henry III a one-tenth for three years, by Pope Innocent IV, we find that the value of the Horseheath title was then fifteen marks. This valuation, the Norwich Taxation, remained the basis of all taxations until about the year 1291[1], when Pope Nicholas IV made a grant of a tithe of all ecclesiastical benefices to King Edward I towards the expenses of a Crusade, for which grant a new valuation was made. By it we find that Horseheath rectory was valued at £10. 13s. 4d., the equivalent of sixteen marks. At this time Horseheath parish contributed a certain yearly amount of support to four religious houses, the value of which to Thorney Abbey, Cambridgeshire, amounted to twelve shillings. Waltham Abbey, Essex, received from its tenants in Horseheath goods to the value of four shillings and sixpence. Hatfield Priory, Hertfordshire, received goods valued at three shillings and twopence, and the Priory of Ely received goods valued at three shillings per annum.

About fifty years after this valuation was made, when King Edward III assumed the title of King

[1] *Taxatio Ecclesiasticus*, 1291.

of France, parliament granted him the ninth lamb, fleece and sheep for two years, towards paying for the expense of the French and Scotch Wars. Owing to the increase in the value of money this one-ninth was considered equivalent to the one-tenth of the 1291 Valuation, upon which the taxation of one-ninth was based for King Edward III. The returns of the Cambridgeshire Commissioners, William le Moigne and Hugh de Croft, for this tax are given in the *Nonae Rolls*[1] and reveal the state of poverty in the county, caused by the already heavy taxation. As far as Horseheath is concerned, the Commissioners state that the ninth in this parish does not come up to the required amount based on the 1291 Valuation, when the rectory was taxed at £10. 13s. 4d., because some of that tax came from church endowments, and other commodities, valued at four pounds, thirteen shillings, and fourpence. The Commissioners also report that two hundred acres of arable land lay uncultivated. Therefore the actual value of the ninth was—on the oaths of twelve jurors—stated to be thirteen shillings and fourpence—one mark.

In 1535, at the time of the Reformation, a survey of all ecclesiastical property was again made. The first-fruits and tenths were now no longer sent to Rome, but were transferred to the Crown. By this *Valor Ecclesiasticus*[2] of King Henry VIII, the rectory of Horseheath is stated to be worth £13. 6s. 8d., the tenth of which, six shillings and eightpence, went to the Crown.

---

[1] *Inquisitiones Nonarum*, p. 313.

[2] Vol. III. p. 504.

With reference to glebe land we find that about
forty years after this valuation, according to a Terrier
made in 1574[1], that there were apparently twenty
acres and one and a half roods of glebe belonging
to Horseheath rectory. This acreage of glebe represents thirty-two separate pieces of land, most of
which was in half-acre strips, but varying in size from
a rood to two acres, chiefly scattered about the open
fields. This one piece of two acres was pasture land
adjoining the rectory. The position of some of these
thirty-two pieces of land gives us some idea of the
difficulty the rectors must of necessity have had in
farming their glebe. And the tithable land, equally
scattered in the open fields, must have required exceedingly careful supervision, especially when at that
time all tithes were paid in kind. Of this twenty
acres of glebe land in Horseheath belonging to the
rector, one half acre of it was in Tosebrook field, a
mile south of the rectory. There were ten pieces in
Chalkesly field, some of which lay fully a mile and a
half south-west of the rectory. In Stonefield, east of
the Bartlow Balk, there were five pieces, some of which
were about two miles south of the rectory. In Crow
Croft, about a mile in the same direction, there were
eight pieces. Then there were the small pieces of
land in the open fields which lay south-east of the
rectory and about the same distances away, the
land nearer the rectory in this direction being park
land.

In 1638[2] the amount of glebe was estimated to be
about twenty-two acres. According to a Terrier dated

[1] Ely, *Terriers*, J. 1.   [2] *Terriers*, J. 1.

the twentieth of March 1692[1], the glebe was then
stated to be twenty-three acres and three and a half
roods. By this Terrier we find that there was a
custom at Horseheath of taking the tithe of barley
rakings, and of paying nine days' cheese for the tithe
of the dairies, for the months of May, June and July,
that is to say, nine days' produce of cheese from the
dairies during those three months. Tithe to the value
of one shilling and twopence was paid on the Old
Park, and on five closes by Horseheath Hall. The
tithe from the windmill at this time was three shillings
and fourpence. One shilling was chargeable yearly
on a close of eight acres called Claydon's Close in
Shudy Camps parish. Caleman's Close in the same
parish, probably a piece of land held by John Caleman,
who died in 1402[2], was chargeable with sixpence.

In 1745[3] the value of Horseheath rectory was
about one hundred pounds. In 1758[4] the tithe
amounted to one hundred and twenty-five pounds.
Of this sum, thirty-one pounds sixteen shillings and
ninepence was paid by the lord of the manor, Lord
Montfort. A dove-house in Horseheath yielded one
pound and one shilling. There was in addition some
tithe from the chestnut and oak trees in Haycroft, as
well as from the spring wood that grew round this
field, in the adjoining parish of Streetly End, next to
Streetly Hall. The wood round this field was felled
about every twelve years and was paid in kind, but
in the year 1769[5] the sum of one pound, one shilling,
was paid instead of wood.

[1] *Terriers*, J. 1.   [2] *Inq. Post Mortem*, 4 Hen. IV, No. 2.
[3] *Addit. MS.* 5808.   [4] *Papers at Horseheath Rectory.*   [5] *Id.*

A further source of income in 1758 came from pigs, it being the custom at Horseheath, instead of contributing pigs in kind to the rector, to make a payment of twopence for each pig, few or many pigs. Apart from tithe, another small source of income at this time were the rector's fees or oblations, which were as follows[1]:—

	£	s.	d.
For publishing Banns	o	1	6
For Marriage by Banns	o	2	6
For Certificate of Publishing Banns	o	1	6
For searching the Register and Certificate of Age	o	o	6
„ „ „ „ „ Marriage	o	1	o
For burying a parishioner	o	2	o
„ one from another parish	–	–	–
For Breaking ground . . . . . 6s. 8d.			
Double fee . . . . 4s. od.	o	10	8
For setting up a gravestone or board	o	6	8
For burying in the chancel or church	–	–	–
„ „ family vault	–	–	–

Certain fees that would concern the wealthier parishioners appear to have been left an open question. Philip Bearcroft, rector, in 1770 states that the fee of sixpence for the Churching of Women by a most extraordinary custom, peculiar perhaps to Horseheath, was received by the parish clerk for his own use.

In 1771[1] the tithable land in Horseheath yielded the rector an income of one hundred and twenty-one pounds, nine shillings, and ninepence. The tithe from one thousand eight hundred and sixty-two acres of land in Horseheath in 1826[1] was valued at three hundred and eighty-one pounds. The lord of the manor, Stanlake Batson, farmed about four hundred

[1] *Papers at Horseheath Rectory.*

and twenty acres of this amount himself, and William Sanxter, the largest tenant farmer, farmed nearly eight hundred acres.

According to an Act of Parliament in 1839, the great and small tithe belonging to Horseheath rectory was commuted for the sum of three hundred and eighty-five pounds, and sixty-five pounds Poor Rate[1]. Tithe, great and small, from twenty-five acres of land in Shudy Camps was at the same time commuted for seven pounds, four shillings, and sixpence. Horseheath rectory tithe has now decreased.

Whilst taking into consideration the relative value of money, perhaps at no time was the value of Horseheath rectory greater than during the years 1847–73, when the yearly income amounted to about five hundred and forty pounds. Shortly after this date it fell to about four hundred pounds, and at the present time it is reduced to three hundred and twenty-seven pounds. The rental of fifteen acres of glebe brings in an additional twenty pounds ten shillings.

The tithe barn stood on a piece of ground, now used as a garden, adjoining the north side of the churchyard, by the road from Horseheath to West Wickham. A faculty for its destruction is dated the ninth of April, 1881. The school, which stood in the churchyard near this barn, was pulled down in 1876. The material was sold to Luke King, of Haverhill, for eighteen pounds.

[1] *Papers at Horseheath Rectory* (Terrier).

CHAPTER VI

THE RECTORS

THE Registers of the Diocese of Ely do not begin until the year 1337, and, since several Registers are missing, it is somewhat difficult to compile a satisfactory

CENTURY	NAME	APPOINTED
xiij	Master Roger	1234, R. here
	Simon de Nosterfield	1298, R. here
xiv	John Cole	was R. here
	William de Bingham	1347, 28 March
	Richard de Preston	1349, 15 July
	John de Horsham	1349, 30 July
	Richard Edmond	c. 1378
	Henry de Hamerton	1386, 28 Nov.
	Thomas Martyn	1395, 31 Oct.
xv	William Buckworth	c. 1416
	John Turnour	1455, 12 June
	John Hopton	1474, 1 March
xvj	Henry Goodwyn	1500, 7 April
	Dns. John...	1518, R. here
	William Masterson	1518
	Thomas White, S.T.B.	1556
	Thomas Wakefield, M.A., S.T.B.	1589, 26 May
xvij	Thomas Wakefield, M.A.	1626, 18 Dec.
	William Eedes, M.A.	1668, 5 March
xviij	Edward Basset, M.A., LL.D.	1709, 7 July
	Thomas Rowell, S.T.B.	1732, 21 Oct.
	Roger Barker, M.A.	1737, 8 Jan.
	Philip Bearcroft, M.A.	1758, 8 Feb.
	" "	1759, 31 Aug.
	John Maule, M.A.	1776, 29 May
xix	Thomas Cozens Percival, M.A.	1825, 2 March
	William Battiscombe, M.A.	1848, 19 May
	James Butter, M.A.	1873, 12 March
	John James Myrton Cunynghame, M.A.	1875, 13 Sept.
	Charles Alexander Borrer, B.A.	1885, 10 Dec.
xx	Edward Joseph Green, M.A.	1909, 2 Nov.

list of the Rectors of Horseheath[1]. In the list of thirty rectors whose names we have been able to give, the succession is complete where the brackets occur.

AUTHORITY	PATRONS	VACATES
Ely Ep. Records, Liber M, p. 481	—	—
Assize Roll, Cambs. 96	—	—
Bp Insula's Register	—	1347, Exchange
„ „	John, Earl of Oxford	—
„ „	„ „	—
East Anglian, Vol. 8, p. 173	„ „	1386, Died
Bp Arundel's Register	Elizabeth de Vere	1395, Resigned
Bp Fordham's Register	Aubrey, Earl of Oxford	
Pat. Roll, 4 Henry V, No. 17, m. 24	? Richard, Earl of Oxford	1455, Died
Bp Gray's Register	John, Earl of Oxford	1474, „
	Richard, Duke of Gloucester	1500, Resigned
Bp Alcock's Register	John, Earl of Oxford	—
Bp's Visitation Bk. 1518	—	—
„ „	—	1556, Died
Baker MS. xxviij. 295	John, Earl of Oxford	1589, „
Lambeth Register	Robert Bentley and Richard Worlich	1626, „
Parish Register	William George	1668, „
„ „	Governors of Charterhouse	1709, „
„ „	„ „	1732, Cessed
„ „	„ „	1737, Died
„ „	„ „	1758, Cessed
„ „	„ „	
„ „	„ „	1776, Died
„ „	„ „	1825, „
„ „	„ „	1848, Cessed
„ „	„ „	1873, Died
„ „	„ „	1875, Cessed
„ „	„ „	1885, Died
„ „	„ „	1909, Resigned
Parish Magazine	„ „	

[1] We are indebted to Canon Crosby for the names of Master Roger 1234, and Dns. John 1518, and other details relating to the Rectors.

The first name on the list, Master Roger, has the distinction of being one of the rectors who undoubtedly officiated in the Norman church.

Simon de Nosterfield, or de Camps, as he was sometimes called, was a son of Nicholas de Nosterfield[1]. This surname is taken from the end-ship called Nosterfield, mentioned in Domesday. Nosterfield was separately taxed in 1250[2], but subsequently was merged into the parish of Shudy Camps, adjoining Horseheath on the south. Simon de Nosterfield first comes to our notice in 1298[3], when he bought four pieces of land in Horseheath, from William le Harpour. This local rector was evidently anxious to acquire property in Horseheath. About the year 1307[4], Henry le Newman sold him a piece of arable land in Hallfield, and Simon Bernard, of Northo, sold him three and a half acres of arable land for forty shillings. About the same time his brother, William de Nosterfield, sold him an annuity of a halfpenny, for one mark, out of land in Nosterfield[5]. This rector's name occurs in conjunction with several others, whom Baldwin de Manners accused of breaking his houses at Horseheath, and taking away his trees and timber, in the year 1310[6]. Perhaps this rector died without a will. In any case, twenty-three pieces of his arable land descended to his brother William, his heir-at-law. This

[1] *Addit. MS.* 5823, f. 223.
[2] *The East Anglian*, Vol. VI. p. 266.
[3] *Addit. MS.* 5823, f. 246.
[4] *Id.* f. 258.   [5] *Id.* f. 223.
[6] *Patent Roll*, 1310, memb. 4 d. In 1279 Baldwin de Manners had six tenants in Horseheath, and held a manor in Fulbourn, and Yen Hall, West Wickham, Cambs. *Hundred Roll*.

land William de Nosterfield sold in 1314[1] to Richard de Horseth, who held land under the Earl of Oxford. Simon de Nosterfield's gifts to Horseheath Church have already been mentioned in dealing with the Church Furniture.

John Cole, who exchanged the Horseheath living with William de Bingham, rector of ? Cottisgrave, Lincolnshire, was from Newport Pagnell, Buckinghamshire[2].

William de Bingham had been rector of Brandon from 1317 to 1324. He had also held the rectory of S. Edward's, Cambridge, and the rectory of Risington, Gloucestershire[3].

Presentations to the Horseheath living about this time occur in rapid succession. Possibly both William de Bingham and his successor, Richard de Preston, appointed in 1349, were victims of the Black Death as about a fortnight after Richard de Preston's appointment the living was given to John de Horsham, who, on the eighteenth of November, 1352, was granted a licence for absence[4]. John de Horsham was subsequently rector of ? Derton, and of Brinton, Norfolk, but he was still rector of Horseheath in the year 1360[5], when, by a deed of that date, he and Simon Ailward granted John Caleman, a smith of Horseheath, a croft in Horseheath which they held of the gift of Adam Lyon. This smith also held land at Shudy Camps. (See page 63.)

[1] *Addit. MS.* 5823, f. 229.
[2] *Bp de Insula's Register*, f. 9 b.
[3] *Bp Montacute's Register*, f. 26 b.
[4] *Bp de Insula's Register*, f. 44 b. [5] *Addit. MS.* 5823, f. 259

From the Poll Tax of 1378, we find that Richard
Edmond was taxed at five shillings on twenty pounds[1].
In 1381[2] this rector purchased one-fifth part of a messuage and two hundred acres of land, ten acres of
meadowland, and thirty acres of pasture in Horseheath,
Shudy Camps, Nosterfield and Castle Camps, for thirty
marks, from John Stukely and his wife, Dionisia, of
Saffron Walden, Essex. This property yielded a
yearly rental of twenty shillings.

In March, four months after Henry de Hamerton's
appointment to Horseheath rectory in 1386, he was
granted a licence for an absence of two years, to
attend Lady Luterall, sister of the Archbishop of
Canterbury[3]. Hamerton was probably a protégé of the
Earl of Oxford, and evidently in great favour with the
authorities since he was appointed rector before he was
ordained in June, 1387. He became Prebendary of
Hereford, and on the twenty-ninth of September,
1390[4], he again obtained a licence for three years'
absence.

In 1416[5] William Buckworth obtained three roods
of land that belonged to William Alington to enlarge
the rectory garden. This rector's name frequently
occurs in connection with various trusteeships of the
Alington property between the years 1428 and 1454[6].
On his death in the following year, 1455[7], the year

---

[1] *The East Anglian*, Vol. XIII. p. 173.
[2] *Feet of Fines*, 5 Ric. II, No. 28.
[3] *Bp Arundel's Register*, f. 59 b.
[4] *Bp Fordham's Register*, f. 12 b.
[5] *Patent Roll*, 4 Hen. V, memb. 24.
[6] *Addit. MS.* 5823.
[7] *Bp Gray's Register*, f. 10.

when the Wars of the Roses began, John Turnour
was appointed to the Horseheath living by John de
Vere, the twelfth Earl of Oxford, the patron who,
owing to his loyalty to King Henry VI, was beheaded
in 1461. John Turnour's name occurs in the marriage
settlement, dated 1468[1], of William Alington and his
second wife, Elizabeth Sapcote.

On the death of John Turnour, John Hopton was
appointed to the Horseheath vacancy in March, 1474[2],
by Robert Cowper, acting as proxy for Richard, Duke
of Gloucester, to whom the Earl of Oxford's escheated
estates had been granted by the King. After holding
the living for twenty-six years, John Hopton was
succeeded by Henry Goodwyn in 1500[3]. He was
appointed by John de Vere, the thirteenth Earl of
Oxford, the de Vere property having been restored
at the termination of the Wars of the Roses.

From the appointment of William Masterson in
1518, the succession of Horseheath rectors is complete up to the present day. William Masterson
was probably presented to the living by John, the
fourteenth Earl of Oxford, who, on account of his
dwarfness, was often styled Little John, of Camps,
where he sometimes resided. It was William Masterson,
with his mobile turn of mind, who shepherded the
Horseheath parishioners through the difficulties of the
Reformation, through the reign of King Edward VI
onwards, towards the close of Queen Mary's reign.
His death in 1556, saved him a further readjustment

[1] *Addit. MS.* 5823, f. 223.
[2] *Bp Gray's Register*, f. 91 b.
[3] *Bp Alcock's Register*, f. 136.

of his religious principles, which would have been necessary in the following reign. This rector's name frequently occurs during his incumbency as witness to the wills of his parishioners, William Sloo's will, dated the fifth of November 1518[1], being the earliest will we have found witnessed by him. His name also occurs in various legal transactions relating to property belonging to the Alington family[2].

This rector's will[3], of which we here print an abstract, gives us some idea of his worldly goods. We regret that he did not give the titles of the small books that Thomas Jaggard was to use for his education :—

"William Masterson, Clerk of Horseth. In the name of God Amen. 20 June 1556. I William Masterson, Clerk and parson of Horseheath, bequeath my soul to Almighty God and to our Ladie S. Mary and my body to be buryed in the Chauncell or Church of All Hallows of Horseth. Item. I bequeath to the Church of Ely xii^d. Item. to Mr Carter my black gowne furred and my joyned bedd, as it standethe hole in the parlere, and my cubbord in the same place. I bequeath to Symon Mosse a bedd wth two pairs of sheets, and foure markes in money if he go forward in lernynge. Item. I give to Thomas Jaggard xx^s. Item. I give to William Cokerton iii^s iiii^d. Item. I give to Richard Cokerton li^n iiii^d. Item. I give to John Smythe and his wyef if they continue with me, a bedde with two pairs of sheets, and ii^s of money. Item. I bequeath to John Cokerton,

---

[1] *Addit. MS.* 5861, f. 125.   [2] *Addit. MS.* 5823.
[3] *Cons. Court of Ely*, N. f. 216.

a matresse a bolster, and a payr of sheets, a payr of
blanketts and a coverlett. Item. to Richard Cokerton
a matresse, a bolster, a payer of sheets, a payer of
blanketts and a coverlett. Item. I give to James
Masterson and his wife, my rayment that is not bequeathed, and to everie one of their children xii^d,
and to my neyce phylyce sayre, my cupboard that
standeth in the hawle. Item. I give to the Church
of Horseheath aforesaid x^li. Item. I will that
Mr Carter and Symon Mosse have my books, so
that Sr. Tomson of Clare Hall have my booke called
Catena Aurea[1], and my booke *Sancti Thomae Aquini
super epistolas pauli*, and Thomas Jagard have such
small bookes as be inew for his learnying. Item. I
give and bequeath to my brother, James Masterson,
my vi sylver spoones and fether bedde, and xx^s in
money. The residue of my gooddes above not bequeathed, my debts paid, my funeralty, my vii^th daie,
and moneth daie performed, to be divided amongst
the poor within the aforesaid parish of Horseheath
at the discretion of John Webb and William Curteys,
whome I ordayne and make my executors, and these
to have for their paynestakying, either of them x^s.
Hiis testibus, Sr. Tomson, scoler of Clare Hall, John
Pomell and Henry Salmon. Probatum 15 January
1556."

In dealing with the Advowson we have already
stated that there were two claimants when the living
became vacant on the death of William Masterson in
1556. The Dowager Countess of Oxford claimed the
right to present Richard Chapman, and John, the

[1] Also by St Thomas Aquinas.

sixteenth Earl of Oxford, recognised to be the lawful owner, presented Thomas White, who had the reputation of being a good preacher. At the time of his appointment, towards the end of Queen Mary's reign, Thomas White must have been a Catholic, but he became a Protestant on the accession of Queen Elizabeth, though, it appears, not so good a Protestant as required by Ecclesiastical law. Otherwise he would not have been presented in 1564[1] for not reading the *Homilies* to his parishioners, as he ought to have done. Neither did he distribute the fourteenth part of his benefice. But if the parson found it difficult to conform to everything required by the changes in religion, surely the parishioners found it an equally difficult matter, several of whom, as late as 1580[2], still made their genuflexion to the churchyard cross, thereby being the means of its removal, in order to put a stop to their idolatry. Without the aid of a Register, we are inclined to think that enforced attendance at church must have been a tax on the memory of those in charge of such affairs. Thomas White appears to have been supported by extremely zealous churchwardens, who took every opportunity of bringing offenders to task, but sometimes exposing a certain amount of pettiness, as in the case of William Curtis, a servant of Sir Giles Alington, who was continually being presented for non-attendance at his parish church, and for not receiving the Communion. In 1580[2], after causing the churchwardens a considerable amount of vexation, Curtis explained to the

---

[1] *Visitation Book*, B. 3.
[2] *Consistory Court Book*, D.

Ecclesiastical Court, that the affair was but a money matter, that when his master attended the parish church, he attended the parish church with his master. But when his master had service or prayers at his own house, Horseheath Hall, he naturally attended service there with his master.

Our attention is drawn to some of Thomas White's refractory parishioners, by a document amongst the State Papers. On the information of Philip Curtis, in August, 1586[1], a man, named Alan Chapman, was brought before two of the Justices of the Peace for Cambridgeshire—Robert Taylor, and Robert Millicent, esquire, of Linton—for aiding the Queen's enemies, the Jesuit priests, and for being friendly with Sir Thomas, a seminary priest. It was further stated that this man gave assistance to Doctor Laurence Webb, general Confessor at Rheims, by the aid of two men, named Mooney and Scott, and a seminary priest who had a "stump foot," named Philip Parker, by sending messages into their country. Except for admitting that he once met the man named Mooney, without knowing him to be a priest, Alan Chapman denied all the charges against him. Dr Webb's sister, Joan Curtis, and her niece Margaret, the wife of Robert Pomell, resided at Carbonells, Horseheath, a moated residence at one of the highest points in Cambridge-shire.

Thomas Wakefield the next rector was born at Radwinter, Essex, on the sixteenth of June, 1560[2]. Robert Bentley and Richard Worlich, *alias* Mynott,

---

[1] P. R. O. *State Papers Domestic*, Elizabeth, Vol. 192.
[2] Durham Cathedral Library, *Hunter MS.* 74.

husband of Dionisia, who appointed Thomas Wakefield to the Horseheath living in 1589, were the executors of Philip Mynott. This rector came to the parish at a time when the country was still rejoicing over the escape from Romish domination by the defeat of the Great Armada. He apparently devoted himself to the improvement of his family fortune by buying and selling land, and by lending money to his ambitious neighbours.

In 1591[1] Thomas Wakefield was presented for not wearing his surplice on Sundays and for neglecting to make good the dilapidation made by the Reformers in the church. We find that Thomas Wakefield lent one hundred pounds to a man named Simon Adams, of Hadstock, Essex, for ten years at the rate of fifteen per cent., on twenty acres of land in Horseheath and Hadstock. This Simon's father, a yeoman of Horseheath, had previously borrowed a hundred pounds on the same land from the rector, which hundred the son still owed, in addition to the further advancement of one hundred pounds. The rector also leased seven acres of land in Horseheath and Shudy Camps to Simon Adams, senior, in 1620[2], for ten years at a rental of fifteen pounds a year. By an indenture, made the thirteenth of March 1619[3], Richard Cockerton and Thomas Wakefield, clerk, sold Sir Giles Alington a messuage in Horseheath, with a toft, called .Francis Garden, and Revels-pightell, containing about three roods, for eighty pounds.

In dealing with the Advowson, we have already

---

[1] *Visitation Book*, B. 2.   [2] Deed *penes* C. E. P.
Addit. MS. 5823, f. 253.

seen, by Thomas Wakefield's will, the provision made by him to secure the Horseheath living for his son Thomas; and the Wakefield memorial tablet, on the north wall of the chancel, has been mentioned in dealing with the Monuments.

Thomas Wakefield, son of the foregoing, was baptized in Horseheath Church on the twenty-eighth of October, 1600[1]. He was ordained on the fifth of March, 1625[2], and, in accordance with the wish expressed in his father's will, was, upon his death in 1626[3], presented to Horseheath rectory by William George. A memorandum in the Parish Register, dated the thirty-first of December 1626, states that "Thomas Wakefield lately inducted rector of the Church of Horseheath, did the day and year above written read the Articles agreed upon by the Archbishop and Bishops of both Provinces, and the whole clergy in the convocation held at London in the year 1562, in the said parish church of Horseheath, and did thereunto declare his free and full assent and consent. Witnesses. Robert Allen, John Adams, Richard Webb." This rector, inducted when twenty-six years of age, ministered to the parishioners of Horseheath in troublesome times, being rector in the reign of King Charles I and also during the Commonwealth, and in part of the reign of King Charles II, evidently accommodating himself with ease to the changes of political opinion. Though Episcopally ordained and instituted, he appears to have had a weakness for Puritanism.

[1] *Horseheath Parish Register.*
[2] *Visitation Book*, B. 3.   [3] *Lambeth Register*, f. 324 a.

For instance, his negligence in wearing a surplice at the Sacrament of Baptism comes to our notice in 1639[1], and later on, in 1662[2], he offends by wearing white stockings and a white cap, contrary to the Articles. Apparently he became lax with regard to the upkeep of the church and rectory. From the Archdeacon's Visitation of 1662, we find that the rectory dove-house had fallen down owing to his neglect, and that he allowed his hogs and cows to graze in the churchyard. In 1636[3] we find him rated to find one musket furnished. About the year 1660[4] his Poll Tax was £2. 13s. 8d. Owing to an illness in 1663, this rector made his will[5], in the usual pious form of that period. He lived, however, until 1668, and was buried on the fourth of February, at Horseheath, having been rector of the parish for about forty-two years.

His will is as follows : " In the name of God Amen. The thirteenth day of January in the year of our Lord one thousand six hundred and sixty-three. I Thomas Wakefield of Horseheath, in the county of Cambridge, within the Diocese of Ely, Clerk, finding myself something ill in body, but of perfect mind and memory to be certaine of all, and the houre of death uncertaine, Doe in the Consideraçon thereof, (as alsoe for the avoydance of all further troubles, suits and Controversies, that otherwise for want of a will might happen between my wife and children) make and ordeine this my last will and Testament, in manner following, hereby revoking and utterly renouncing all

---

[1] *Visitation Book*, B. 3.   [2] *Id.* 1662, B. 3.
[3] Bodleian Library, *Rawlinson MS.* B. 278.
[4] P. R. O. *Lay Subsidy*, $\frac{81}{127}$.   [5] *Cons. Court of Ely*, Bury, f. 81.

other, and former wills whatsoever by me heretofore
made, ffirst and principally I comend, and with a ffree
Hearte render againe my Soule into the hands of
Almighty God that gave it, hopeing assuredly through
the meritts, death and passion of Jesus Christ, my only
Saviour and Redeemer, to have my sinns pardoned
and my soul eternally saved. My Body I bequeath
to the earth from whence it first came, to be decently
and Christianlike buried in the chancell of Horseheath
aforesaid att the discretion of my executors heretofore
named. And as for that porčon of outward estate
which it hath pleased God of his mercy to bestow
upon me, I dispose of as followeth. ffirst I give and
bequeath all those ffreehold houses, lands and Tena-
ments whatsoever situate, lying and being in Castle
Camps, in the County of Cambridge aforesaid, and in
the occupation of Thomas Browne, his assignee or
assignes, imediately after the death of Mary my wife,
to Philip Wakefield my sonne, his heirs and assignes
forever, upon condičon that the said Philip my sonne,
his heirs or assignes shall pay, or cause to be paid,
out of the said Land the summe of Six Hundred and
Twenty Pounds of Lawful money, within three years
after the death of the said Mary, my wife (viz.) the
summe of three score pounds parte thereof to Judith
Wakefield my daughter, and the said summe of threescore pounds to Elizabeth my daughter, the sevall
payments, to be made at, or in, the South porch of
the parish church of Horseheath aforesaid. And my
will and mind is, that in case default of payment shall
be made, of the payment of the said sevall sumes of
threescore pounds apiece, to my said two daughters,

soe bequeathed aforesaid, contrary to the true intent
and meaning of this my last will, that, then it shall
and may be lawfull, to and for my said two daughters,
or either of them, their or either of their Execute^rs or
assignes into all, or any part of the said p^rmisses, to
re-enter, and the same to have and enjoy till the said
sume of One Hundred and twenty Pounds, together
with the arrears thereof (if any be) and all manner
of charges that they or either of them shall be putt
to in the prosecuting of the business, be fully satisfied
and paid.   Item. I give my coppyhold Lands and
Tenem^ts in the occupation of the said Thomas Browne,
and Containing by estimacõn Eighteen Acres, more
or lesse, to my said sonne Philip and his heirs, upon
condicion also, that my said sonne his heirs or assignes
shall pay thereout to my said two daughters the sume
of fforty pounds apeece w^thin three years after my
decease, at, or in the South porch of the parish church
of Horseheath aforesaid, and for want of payment of
the said sume of fforty pounds apeece, to either of
my said daughters, att the time and place aforesaid,
I give and bequeath the said Coppiehold Lands w^th
the appurtenances to my said two daughters Judith
and Elizabeth, and their heirs forever.   Item. I
give to the said Phillip my sonne and his heirs
One acre of Land more or less lyeing in Castle
Camps aforesaid neere Westoe Lay, which is in the
occupacõn of Henry Webb.   Alsoe ffower Acres and
Three Roodes of Land beeing of severall peeces,
and lyeing within the þish of Ashdon in the county
of Essex, I give unto my said sonne Phillip and
his heirs forever.   Item. Those Coppyhold Lands and

Tenements whatsoever lying and being in Castle
Camps aforesaid, and in the occupation of one,
Thomas Allington, I give and bequeath unto Richard
Landsdale, Thomas Wakefield my kinsman and John
Pettitt of Horseheath aforesaid, and their heirs to the
use and behoofe of Thomas Quartus Wakefield my
sonne, and his heirs, the said ffeoffees to receive the
profitts and rents of the said Lands during all the
naturall life of the said Thomas my sonne, towards
the payment of the ffine, and towards the maintenance
of the said Thomas. Item. I will and bequeath to
Nathaniell Wakefield my sonne, all my books, paying
thereout to my said two daughters ffive pounds apiece
within one year after my decease. Item. I give and
bequeath to Mary my daughter ffive pounds to be
paid her by my said Executor within three months
after my decease. I give unto my servant William
Wright Twenty shillings over and above his wages.
Item. I give unto my said son Thomas Quartus
two of my best silver spoons with knobbs. Item. All
other my moveable goods, chattels and household
stuffe whatsoever, I give to my loving wife and my
said two daughters, Judith and Elizabeth, to be de-
vided amongst them in manner following (that is to
say) the one half part thereof to Mary my wife, and
the other half thereof to my said two daughters. And
in case either of my said daughters Judith or Elizabeth
shall happen to depart this life before the Legaceys
or porčons soe given as aforesaid be due or unpaid,
that then my will is, that the sister surviving shall
have the Legaceys or porčons of the deceased. And
I doe hereby make and ordeine Mary my deare wife

sole executrix of this my last will, and I doe also nominate my very good ffriend Richard Lansdale to be supͮvisor of this my said will requesting him to see this my said will carefully performed, and for his paynes therein, I give him fforty shillings. In wittness whereof I the said Thomas Wakefield have hereunto sett my hand and seale the day and year first above written, 1663. Thomas Wakefield. Read, sealed, subscribed, declared, published, and acknowledged to be the last will and Testament of the said Thomas Wakefield in the presence of us Robert Poole, John Hayward, Sen.

"Probatum est. Decimo Quinto die mensis Maii A.D. 1669."

There are two commonplace books from Thomas Wakefield's library, which he bequeathed in this will to his son Nathaniel, in Durham Cathedral Library, in the *Christopher Hunter Collection MSS.* No. 19 and No. 74. Both of these volumes contain interesting memoranda of the Wakefield family. One book appears to have been used as a kind of register, and in MS. Number 19, fol. 5 there are the following lines:

"In memory of my grandfather.
" Reader.
"AWAKE, I shall when Christ hath got the FIELD,
Hold fast the fayth, throw not away thy Shield."

Dr W. M. Palmer in the *East Anglian*, Vol. XIII. p. 306, has given an inventory of this rector's goods and chattels at the time of his death. By permission we here reprint this inventory, which gives us an excellent idea of how the rectory was furnished by a prosperous rector in 1668.

Thos. Wakefield, Horseheath, clarke, an Inventory of his Goods and Chattels.

	£	s.	d.
In ready money in his purse	10	0	
His wearing apparal	5	0	0
In Hall: one long table, two formes, one short table, 3 chairs, 7 joined stools, one bench bord, 7 cushions, one presse for cloths, 2 bracelets, one pair of andirons, firepan and tongs, one table carpet, one livery carpet, and one still	3	0	0
In parlour: one table and trand, 6 joined stooles, one elboe chaire, 6 backe chaires, 6 covered stooles of turke worke, one square table, one livery cubbord, 3 cushons, one table carpet, one carpet for a square table, one livery carpet, a pair of andions, fire shovell, tongs, paire of bellows, hangins in parlour, chess bord and chesmen	5	6	8
In parlour chamber: bedsted, fetherbed, 3 blankets, one coverled, 2 bolsters, 4 pillowes, curtains, valance, one elboe chair, 3 back chaires, wecker chaire, 7 low stooles, press for cloths, dust sheet, 3 cushons, oris hangings, press, carpet, truncke, box, joined stoole, bason and ure, 2 candlesticks, one chamber pot, all earthenware, pair of andions, fire shovel, bellows	10	0	0
In Hall chamber: bedsted, fetherbed, 2 bolsters, 2 pillows, 4 blanckets, coverled, curtains, valence, window curtaine, elboe chaire, backe chaire, 5 stools, livery cupbord, deske, cabnett, 2 chests, livery carpet, 4 cushens, cobirons, bellows ...	6	0	0
In Maids' Chamber: posted bedsted, fether bed, 2 blanckets, 2 bolsters, pillow, Rugg, curtains, valance, trundle bed, flocke bed, 2 blankets, bolster and pillow	4	0	0
In Kitchen Chamber: posted bedsted, 3 blankets, 3 bolsters, fetherbed, another fetherbed, rugg, 3 pillows, coverled, bolster, curtains, valence, truncke, closs stool, livery cubbord, wicker chaire, cushen, 2 small stooles, box, pair of andirons, tongs, bellows, fire shovells	7	0	0
In man's chamber: fether bed, flock bed, 3 bolsters, blancket, 2 coverleds, old box, press	2	0	0
In Barn: wheat, barley, Oats, Rye	27	0	0

	£	s.	d.
In Barn: one sercul, bushel, pecke, strike, lader, 10 sacks, a casten shovell, 2 stans		13	4
In Hay Barn: hay	6	13	4
Dung in yard and Cow partes	1	0	0
One macteque, spade, and other things used for husbandry		13	0
5 paire of fine sheets, 10 paire course sheets, 9 paire pellubeers, table cloth of dieper, a dozen dieper napkins, cubbord cloth of same, 2 doz. course napkins, 3 long table cloths, 6 small table cloths, 12 towells	10	0	0
Tillts: 7 ackers and half 4 earth at 4/- the earth[1], 3 ackers strucke	6	6	0
Seaven roods wheate of the above seaven ackers with 3½ bushels wheate		14	0
For plowing oat land 6 akers and three roods	1	7	0
For sed 7 bushels peas 16 bushels oats	1	19	2
For carting 23 load dung and for dung	2	0	0
For 4 flitches bacon	2	0	0
Poultry hens in yard		5	0
10 Silver spoons	3	10	0
2 Silver salts	2	0	0
Chaff and strawe	2	0	0
Debts owing	21	18	7
For goods omitted		10	0
Total[2]	£243	4	9

Ric. Lansdall,
John Haylock,
Adam Blackwall, } Appraisers.
Thomas Wakefield,
Mary Wakefield, Executrix.

Exhibited 13th May, 1668.

[1] A day's ploughing.
[2] The total is thus given in the original, but the different items when added up only come to £133. 6s. 1d. In one part the document is torn, so some portion may be missing. No mention is made of books, but, as noted above, a library is bequeathed in the will, and this ought to have been and probably was included in the complete inventory.

William Eedes, a member of Christ's College,
Cambridge, has the distinction of being the first
rector of Horseheath who was appointed by the
Governors of Charterhouse. The presentation was
made on the fifth day of March, 1668[1]. After an
incumbency of over thirty years, William Eedes died
at Horseheath at the age of sixty-eight, on the third
of April, 1709. He was buried on the twenty-ninth
of the same month. In dealing with the Monuments
we have already referred to the mural tablet erected
to his memory on the north wall of the chancel. His
wife was buried in S. Andrew's Church, Cambridge[2].
Before his appointment to Horseheath rectory, William
Eedes was a curate at Fen Drayton, Cambridgeshire.
Cole has said of him that he was an odd kind of man ;
he held the rectory in the reign of King Charles II,
James II, during the Revolution of 1688, also in the
reign of William and Mary, and part of Queen Anne's
reign. Although it is stated that there were no pro-
fessed papists in Horseheath parish when William
Eedes was rector, still there were several Non-con-
formists, amongst them a Quaker named Walter Crane,
who, in 1663, was sent to prison for sixteen months for
refusing to pay tithe. He also held meetings in his
house. The Conventicle Act would necessitate a
careful watch over these. Beside non-attendance
at the parish church, burials in private gardens[3], and
non-payment of tithe, were matters which could not
be overlooked. Among his various clerical duties,
we find that this rector, on the twentieth of October,

[1] *Horseheath Parish Register.*   [2] *Addit. MS.* 5808, f. 170.
[3] *Visitation Book,* 1662–8, B. 3.

1672[1], with the churchwardens and overseers, testifying to the Justices of the Peace for the county, that there were ten persons in Horseheath whose rent was not more than twenty shillings per annum, and whose respective houses had but two chimneys, fire-hearths or stoves. Consequently, these persons were exempt from Hearth Tax.

From William Eedes's will[2] made about five years before his death, we see that he owned property in Horseheath, Hildersham, and Helion Bumpstead, and that he had lent money on land in Balsham. Apparently he was not living at the rectory at the time of his death, since the house in which he resided is bequeathed to his daughter. Under his will he makes provision for his wife, and his three daughters, Dorothy —his sole executrix, Alice and Katherine. The estate bequeathed to his son Francis is chargeable with an annuity of twenty pounds for his daughter Alice. This rector left the sum of forty shillings to the poor of Horseheath, and made special provision for the aged poor, for whom he left ten pounds to the minister and churchwardens of Horseheath, to be put out at interest, and William Eedes made it specially clear, that the yearly profit from this sum was to be spent according to his wish, and not in such manner as we think the trustees might have been tempted to administer his charity—by lessening the parish rates. Other bequests are enumerated in the following abstract of the will. Possibly some reader may be able to discover the portrait of his daughter.

[1] P. R. O. *Lay Subsidy*, $\frac{84}{440}$ 24 Charles II.
[2] P. P. C. *Lane*, 141.

"19 August, 1704. I William Eedes, of Horseheath, in the county of Cambridge, Clerk,...my body
to be buried at the discretion of my Executors...
I bequeath to my daughter Dorothy Eedes and her
heirs and assignes, all that my messuage or tenement
wherein I now dwell in Horseheath aforesaid with the
orchard, garden and all other the appurtenances whatsoever to the same belonging. To my daughter Alice
Eedes for life an annuity, or a yearly rent charge of
twenty-five pounds, out of my copie lands and tenna-
ments situate in the town, parish, fields or bounds of
Hildersham, holden of the manor of Hildersham, to
be yearly paid by son ffrancis Eedes, his heirs and
assignes, over and besides all taxes and other charges
ordinary and extraordinary...to be paid her yearly at
the feasts of St Michael, the Archangle, and the
Annunction of the Blessed Virgin Mary, by half yearly
payments...and if not paid it shall be lawfull for the
said Alice Eedes to enter upon my said copyhold
lands...I give to my said son ffrancis Eedes, and his
heirs, my lands free and copy in the town, fields or
bounds of Hildersham chargeable to the said annuity.
I do hereby declare that I have made, and passed
a surrenda of all my said copyhold Lands and premises
in Hildersham into the hands of the lord of the manor
of Hildersham, by the hands of the steward of the courts
of the same manor. To my daughter Dorothy Eedes
all my lands and tenement situate in Helions Bumpstead, in the county of Essex, which I lately purchased
of Hannah Smith, widow, and John Wysham, yeoman.
To Ann, my wife, one Bond for the payment of fifty
pounds with interest made to me from Thomas Boyden

of Horningsey, and his son, and all the money due on the same bond, also fifty pounds out of one hundred owing me from Mr John Lindsell, of Horseheath, upon security of copy land in Balsham. To my daughter Katherine Eedes thirty pounds, my best chest of draws, six of my best silver spoons, one feather bed, one boulster, one pair of pillows and pillow beers, two pair of sheets, two of my best pewter dishes, to be taken at her election. To my daughter Alice Eedes three silver spoons, one feather bed, boulster, pair of pillows and pillow beers, two pewter dishes, two pair of sheets and my great Bible. To the poor of Horseheath the sum of forty shillings. I give ten pounds to be paid within one year after my decease to the minister and church-wardens of Horseheath for the use, and towards the relief of the ancient poor people of that town or parish, to be put out at interest for them, or otherwise laid out in lands, and so put out and settled, so that the increase and profits may be yearly forever, well and truly paid, in such portions and manner unto the ancient poor people of Horseheath...but my will expressly is, that the said ten pounds or any part thereof, or the profits thereof, from thence arrising shall not be taken or used for, or towards the putting out or placing forth of any Parish Child or Children, or otherwise employed, than as aforesaid. To Mr Samuel Newton the elder of S. Edward's parish in Cambridge, ten pounds. To my wife I give my Bond of Paul Purchas and his Mother, the sum of ten pounds also. Also to my wife, whatsoever was her own before her marriage with me, and that she hath bought since, with her own money. To my daughter Katherine, I give her own Picture, my clock and all the furniture of my Parlour Chamber, except a chest of draws and my trunk and what shall be therein. The residue of all moneys, debts, goods and estate whatsoever after my debts...be paid, I give to my daughter Dorothy Eedes whom I appoint my sole Executrix...and I appoint Samuel Newton supervisor to this my last will...

Proved 21 June, 1709."

Edward Basset of Trinity College, Cambridge, was the son of a London bookseller[1]. He married a niece of Henry Markham of Little Abington, Cambs, a non-juror. At the time of her marriage this lady was a Presbyterian. There were two daughters of the marriage, one of whom, Cole says, was a woman of genius and a poetess. Her father taught her Latin and Greek, but cultured as she was, she married the Horseheath miller, and her sister married an apothecary of Linton. Beside practically rebuilding the rectory from the ground—which evidently was too dilapidated for his predecessor to live in—Edward Basset raised a considerable sum of money for the reparation of the church. He also made a good garden for the rectory, which probably had undergone little alteration since it was enlarged in 1416. There is little doubt that we are indebted to Edward Basset for the preservation in the rectory staircase window of some of the painted glass from the church, which fortunately was recorded by Cole. It has now disappeared. One shield bore the emblems of the Trinity in sable and argent.

[1] *Addit. MS.* 5808.

The shield of special interest to us to-day bore the Audley arms, gules, fretty, or[1], the same arms as those now in the east window of the chancel, without the bordure. That Edward Basset's work at Horseheath was appreciated, may be seen from such an instance as is shown in the will of Lord Montfort, lord of the manor of Horseheath. This will[2] was proved in 1718, and by it we find that the rector had borrowed money from Lord Montfort, who, however, did not disclose the sum in his will, but bequeathed to the rector the money which he owed him, with an additional sum of twenty guineas. Edward Basset was a Justice of the Peace for the County of Cambridge. In 1732[3], through the influence of Henry Bromley, he exchanged the Horseheath living, then worth about one hundred and thirty pounds per annum—with a population of three hundred and forty-six persons—for the living at Balsham, a larger parish, worth over three hundred a year. He died at Balsham in the year 1749.

Thomas Rowell a member of Corpus Christi College, Cambridge, appointed to the vacancy at Horseheath on the twenty-first of October, 1732[3], was inducted on the twenty-eighth of October in the same year[4]. This rector resided chiefly in London where he held a curacy or lectureship. After holding the living for about five years, he died in London in September, 1737[3], and was buried in London.

---

[1] *Addit. MS.* 5808, f. 175.
[2] P. P. C. *Tennison*, f. 231.
[3] *Addit. MS.* 5808.
[4] *Horseheath Parish Register.*

Roger Barker was a Sussex man and a bachelor. He was educated at Charterhouse and Clare Hall, Cambridge, and was made a fellow of his College. In 1736 he was one of the Moderators of the University, and examined the celebrated antiquary William Cole for his B.A. degree[1]. When rector of Horseheath, Roger Barker held the curacy of the adjoining parish of West Wickham. After an incumbency of about twenty years at Horseheath, this rector in 1758[2] removed to Castle Camps rectory—a living also in the gift of the Governors of Charterhouse—where he died in 1772.

Philip Bearcroft was a son of Doctor Philip Bearcroft, Master of Charterhouse, who wrote *An Historical Account of Thomas Sutton, esquire, and of His Foundation in Charter-House*. Philip Bearcroft was appointed to the Horseheath living on the eighth of February, 1758[2]. He appears to have resigned the living—why we do not know—and to have been re-appointed on the thirty-first of August, 1759. Lord Montfort gave him the curacy of West Wickham. Cole[3] has described Philip Bearcroft as a clever man, with a most ungracious figure and behaviour, and says that for many years he suffered from a complication of infirmities. He died in very poor circumstances at Horseheath, on the first of February, 1776[3], at the age of forty-four years. He was buried in the chancel of Horseheath Church, where there is a memorial stone to his memory.

[1] *Addit. MS.* 5808.
[2] *Horseheath Parish Register.*
[3] *Addit. MS.* 5808.

John Maule, son of Henry Maule and Mary his wife, was born at Huntingdon on the fifth of May, 1748[1]. He was admitted to Charterhouse school in 1762, and went to Cambridge University in 1766. He was appointed rector of Little Wigborough in Essex in 1774, and of Horseheath on the twenty-fifth of May, 1776, being inducted on the ninth of June following[2]. This rector also held the curacy of West Wickham which was usually served at that time by the rectors of Horseheath. John Maule was also chaplain of Greenwich Hospital, and on that account, by licence, he was chiefly non-resident at Horseheath, though from the returns of 1787 we find that he was sometimes resident at Horseheath for six months during the year[3]. At this time a Mr Walker who lived at Abington was his curate, who, for his work at Horseheath and West Wickham, was paid twenty-five pounds a year[4], whilst the rector's income from the Horseheath living alone was about two hundred a year. During the forty-nine years of his incumbency John Maule had frequent changes of curates, and in 1807[5] he had no settled curate at all. John Thornhill of Linton had just resigned. Services at this time were held alternately in the morning and evening on Sundays and other appointed days, at both Horseheath and West Wickham. The Sacrament was administered at Easter, Whitsuntide and Christmas. At Horseheath there were usually about eight

---

[1] Information kindly given by H. S. Wright, Esq., 'Registrar' of Charterhouse.
[2] *Horseheath Parish Register.*
[3] *Ely Diocese Books*, B. 8, 1787.   [4] *Id.*   [5] *Id.* 1807.

communicants. In 1809[1] a resident curate named Lud-
bury resided at the rectory, and in addition to a salary
of fifty pounds per annum, he was allowed to take the
surplus fees. For this salary he did duty at West
Wickham as well as at Horseheath. In 1813[1] John
Maule was paying an unlicensed curate named Segrave,
sixty pounds a year. There was as yet no Sunday
school to superintend at Horseheath, and the children
did not attend church with any regularity. This fault the
rector justly attributed to their parents, whom he could
not prevail upon to subscribe towards a Sunday school.

There is a man now living at Horseheath who has
told us how his father, James Cole, when a boy, joined
in beating the parish bounds when John Maule was
rector. On these expeditions the rector was taken by
the shoulders and feet and vigorously bumped on each
of the boundary posts, and would often implore the
men not to drink at each 'bumping' post, because they
bumped him so hard! This bumping of the rector
naturally caused no little amusement amongst the
rising generation that joined in beating the parish
bounds. Until quite recently a 'bumping' post
remained at the south-eastern extremity of Horseheath parish, by the side of the Withersfield road,
where the County Council have placed their boundary
post. Another 'bumping' post was at the extreme
north-west of the parish, by a field called Mark's
Grave. A third post was on the Bartlow baulk.

According to a mural tablet in Horseheath Church
John Maule was a descendant of the Panmure family

---

[1] *Visitation Papers*, C. 2.

in Scotland.   He died at Bath in 1825, when seventy-seven years of age.

Thomas Cozens Percival, like his predecessor, was a pluralist—in their day such cases were ubiquitous. He held the rectory of Little Gransden, Cambs, from the sixth of June, 1829 to November, 1831[1]. He was Prebendary of Southwell in 1829[1], and subsequently was rector of Barnborough, Yorks, but he chiefly resided at Horseheath.   The rectory underwent considerable repair under this rector, who, in 1829[2], built new stabling of more substantial material than the old one, which was pulled down.   He also built the school —in flint and red-brick, with slate roof—which formerly stood in the churchyard.   That he took a keen interest in the church will be seen by the following letter addressed to the Archdeacon[3]:—

HORSEHEATH,
LINTON. *Dec.* 11. 1826.

Rev[d] Sir.   I am sorry to be under the necessity of troubling you on the subject of the repairs of my church. For notwithstanding the repeated injunctions which you transmitted to the church-wardens of this parish, there is still much remaining to be done in the way of repairs.

It is not however the object of this letter to solicit your immediate interference, as I intend on the return of a more favourable season to call the attention of the principal Parishioners to the subject, and I hope they may be induced to do what I shall propose without the intervention of your authority.   At present I merely wish to know, if you would

[1] Information supplied by Canon Crosby.
[2] *Visitation Articles and Returns*, C. 2.
[3] *Papers at Horseheath Rectory.*

be good enough to inform me whether the church-wardens
obtained your permission at the latter part of the year 1824,
during the Incumbency of my Predecessor, to reduce the
number of church bells from five to four, as this has been
done. And likewise whether I ought not to insist that the
church-wardens restore the Commandments at the East End,
and the sentences in the Body of the church, which have been
removed and obliterated. I should not have delayed taking
the proper steps for enforcing the repairs of my church soon
after my induction, had I not judged it most convenient that
the body of the church and the chancel should be repaired at
the same time. And I have been prevented hitherto doing
anything to the latter, as I have not yet received any part of
the damages awarded by law for the Dilapidation of my
Rectory.

I am, Revd Sir with great respect

Your obed^t and Humble Servt

THOMAS C. PERCIVAL.

After about twenty-three years residence at Horseheath this rector resigned the living in 1848.

William Battiscombe was appointed to Horseheath
rectory in 1848, when the living was worth about five
hundred and forty pounds per annum. In addition
this rector had private means, and his horses—a pair
of greys, a bay mare and a chestnut—are remembered
with pride in the village. This rector added a large
drawing-room to the rectory, and although he lived in
considerable style at Horseheath, on his death his
executors were confronted with a bill for dilapidations
for about a thousand pounds[1]. However, we believe
this figure was afterwards somewhat reduced.

James Butter, an energetic young bachelor with private means, succeeded William Battiscombe. His father was of Faskelly House, Pitlochry, on whose estate is the pass of Killiecrankie. On coming to Horseheath in 1873, James Butter at once set to work and did all necessary repairs to the church and rectory, and in addition, during his short incumbency of two and a half years, he built the present school and school house. He had just obtained a faculty for extensive alterations to the chancel when he resigned the living for one of more activity at Coventry.

John James Myrton Cunynghame, appointed to Horseheath rectory in 1875, did not restore the chancel until the year 1883. He was chiefly non-resident.

Charles Alexander Borrer was appointed to the Horseheath living in 1885. He was instituted by the Archbishop during the vacancy of the See of Ely. This rector restored the nave and south porch of the church, and in addition spent considerable sums of money on the general up-keep of the church fabric. The Guildhall, on glebe land, was also erected during his incumbency, and will be a lasting memorial of the interest he and his family have taken in the parish. His recent resignation—owing to ill-health—is much regretted by all his parishioners.

¹ *Papers at Horseheath Rectory.*

CHAPTER VII

THE CHARITIES

IN the belfry, a charity-board records four charities belonging to the poor of Horseheath. This charity-board, until the restoration of 1891, hung over the vestry door. From the description of these charities on this board, it is a difficult matter to trace the founders of the first two. The four charities are recorded as follows :—

1. Some Person or Persons now unknown gave to the Churchwardens for the time being of the Parish of Horseheath, in trust for the Benefit of the Poor thereof, a piece of land in the parish of Balsham measuring five Acres, one Rood, and thirty Perches.

2. Some Person or Persons now unknown gave to the church warden for the time being of the Parish of Horseheath, in trust for the Benefit of the Poor thereof, four pieces of land in the parish of Linton, measuring altogether six Acres, one Rood, and thirty-five Perches.

3. John Offord gave by will to the Rector for the time being of the parish of Horseheath, in trust for the Benefit of the Poor thereof, the sum of ten pounds directing that the interest arising from it should be annually divided between five poor widows.

4. The sum of five pounds is annually paid by the occupier of Town Green to the Overseer of the Parish for the Benefit of the Parishioners.

> T. C. Percival, *Rector.*
> Wm. Parken, *Churchwarden.*

The rent arising from the land in Balsham is now disbursed at Christmas, with the five pounds paid by the occupier of Town Green—originally given annually by the Lord of the Manor when he enclosed the land in his park, in lieu of the right of pasturage of the parishioners. Five pounds is now chargeable from the tenant of Town Green, but in 1837 it was said to be worth ten pounds. The interest from the land in Linton provides weekly doles of bread for five poor widows. John Offord's charity of ten pounds was lost in the year 1828 when John Maule was rector, and William Sanxter churchwarden, the latter being responsible for the loss, having left Horseheath with the money in hand[1]. Tradition says that the latter absconded with the trust money, as well as that obtained from the sale of one of Horseheath Church bells.

Charities number one and two, usually go by the name of Wakefield's Charity. The land is supposed to have been purchased with fifty pounds bequeathed for a town stack, for the relief of the poor, in accordance with the will of the Rev. Thomas Wakefield, proved on the sixteenth of December, 1626[2]. Under this will the relief should be disbursed at

---

[1] Ely, *Visitation Articles and Returns*, C. 2.
[2] See p. 57.

Christmas and Easter. A memorandum is made in
Hunter MS. 19. p. 2 by the rector's son, Thomas,
also rector of Horseheath, to the effect that he had
distributed twenty shillings to the poor on Monday
in Easter week, 1628, in consideration of fifty pounds
bequeathed by his father, which was not then invested in land. Similar entries are made in this MS.
with the names of the recipients of this charity
up to the year 1631. However, the entry, dated
the eighteenth of April, 1630, states that the money
distributed then, was from the rent of nine acres of
land purchased with the above said money. This
acreage we notice does not correspond with the acreage
given on the charity-board, that the parishioners
of Horseheath call Wakefield's Charity. Matthew
Teversham was the first tenant of the newly acquired
land in Balsham parish, for in the Parish Register
there is the following entry, dated October 17, 1630:
" Received of Mathew Teversham for the second half-
year's rent of the lands hired by him of the townsmen
of Horseheath, and purchased with fifty pounds given
by Thomas Wakefield formerly parson of Horseheath,
received I say the day and year above written for the
second half-year's rent £1. 3. 0, whereof twenty
shillings were given for making the conveighance,
and one shilling and fourpence for cutting down the
thistles in the sayd lands, and one shilling and eight-
pence remaineth to be given to the poore." The first
payment for the second half-year, of £1. 3s. 0d., was
made on 11 April, 1631, and no expenses were deducted.
On the fifth of May, 1669, an entry in the Register
shows that this land had been re-let, and the rent

raised. "Received of Richard Norden the somme of one pound, five shillings, for his half-year's rent due at our Lady last past. Edward Webb, Churchwarden. This parsell of the poore land was let for 12 years begining at 1668."

In the year 1783[1] fifty shillings from the Balsham property were distributed at Easter. Fifty-two shillings from the Linton land were expended in the distribution of bread. Ten shillings—the interest of a principal of ten pounds, John Offord's charity—were given to the poor widows, making a total value of £5. 12s. 0d. for the poor of Horseheath. In 1837 there were a rental of £6 from land in Balsham and £5 from land in Linton.

As we have seen[2], William Masterson, rector of Horseheath, left the residue of his property to the poor, and we frequently meet with other small donations to the poor. Philip Keasar *alias* Webb in 1612[3] bequeathed to the poorest of Horseheath the sum of six and eight-pence yearly on Good Friday, yearly for twenty years after his death. The Parish Register states that "the first payment whereof was made by William Webb his sonne and heire openly in the parish church of Horseheath on the second day of Aprill, in the year of our lord god 1613, and was thus distributed :

To Austin Parker	8*d.*	Widowe Bawd	6*d.*
Thomas Sandar	8*d.*	Widowe Boyden	6*d.*
Nicholas Matheson	8*d.*	Gyles Onyon's Wife	6*d.*
Old John Clements	8*d.*	John Lyng's wife	6*d.*
John Ward's Wife	8*d.*	John Butcher's Wife	4*d.*
Widow Alyn	8*d.*	Widow Colman	4*d.*"

[1] *Rural Dean's Returns*, B. 7. [2] See p. 72.
[3] *Cons. Court of Ely*, Y. f. 203.

Lady Dorothy Alington, the third wife of William, Lord Alington, by her will[1] proved in 1702 bequeathed a legacy of twenty pounds to the poor of Horseheath, and also sixty pounds to buy land. The rent was intended to provide twelve loaves of bread, which were to be given every Sunday morning after service to the twelve poorest people in Horseheath who went to church. Possibly this sixty pounds may have been invested in the Linton land, otherwise we cannot trace the charity.

We have already seen that in 1709 William Eedes, rector of Horseheath, left ten pounds[2], the interest of which was for the benefit of the aged poor, and John Bromley, esquire, left in the year 1718[3], the sum of fifty pounds to the Horseheath poor to be administered by the Minister, Churchwardens and Overseer of Horseheath parish.

We are told by the oldest inhabitants of Horseheath, that formerly there were some alms-houses near the church, by the Church Farm, and that there was another alms-house by the Weaver Pond, nearly opposite the Manor Farm, where there is at the present time a cottage of comparatively recent date. In 1779[4] there was an alms-house in Horseheath, but there was no revenue to keep it up.

[1] P. P. C. *Herne*, f. 70.
[2] See p. 87.
[3] P. P. C. *Tennison*, f. 231.
[4] *Visitation Books*, B. 3.

Printed in the United States
By Bookmasters